I0763043

National Union Executive Committee.

THE PROCEEDINGS

OF THE

National Union Convention

Held at Philadelphia, August 14, 1866.

Compiled and printed by order of the following resolution, offered by the HON. REVERDY JOHNSON, of Maryland, and passed unanimously:

Resolved, That a full and correct Copy of the Proceedings of this Convention be prepared by E. O. PERRIN, Secretary, and certified by the President, for publication by the Resident Executive Committee at Washington.

FIRST DAY.

THE NATIONAL UNION CONVENTION met at 12 o'clock, Tuesday, August 14, 1866, pursuant to call. Hon. A. W. RANDALL, of Wisconsin, at precisely 12, rose and said:

The meeting will now come to order. For the purpose of the temporary organization of this Convention, I propose the name of General JOHN A. DIX, of New York, as chairman. [Cheers.]

The proposition was received with unanimous acclamation. General JOHN A. DIX came forward and said:

SPEECH OF GENERAL DIX.

Gentlemen of the Convention and Fellow-Citizens of the Whole Union—[Applause:]

I return you my sincere thanks for the honor you have done me in choosing me to preside temporarily over your deliberations. I regard it as a distinction of no ordinary character, not only on account of the high personal and political standing of the gentlemen who compose this Convention, but because it is a Convention of the people of all the States of this Union [cheers,] and because we cannot doubt that, if its proceedings are conducted with harmony and good judgment, it will lead to the most important results. It may be truly said that no body of men has met on this continent under circumstances so momentous and so delicate since the year 1787—the year when our ancestors assembled in this city to frame a better government for the States which were parties to the old Confederation—a government which has been confirmed and made more enduring, as we trust, by the fearful trials and perils which it has encountered and overcome. The Constitution which they came here to plan and construct, we are here to vindicate and restore. [Cheers.] We are here to assert the supremacy of representative government over all who are within the confines of the Union—a government which cannot, without a violation of its fundamental principle, be extended over any but those who are represented in it [loud applause]—over those who, by virtue of that representation, are entitled to a voice in the administration of the public affairs. [Renewed applause.] It was such a Government our fathers framed and put in operation. It is the Government which we are bound by every consideration of fidelity, justice, and good faith to defend and maintain. [Cheers.]

Gentlemen, we are not living under such a Government. [Applause and cries of "That is true."] Thirty-six States have for months been governed by twenty-five—eleven States have been wholly without representation in the legislative body of the nation; the numerical proportion of the represented States to the unrepresented has just been changed by the admission of the delegates from Tennessee—a unit taken from the smaller and added to the larger number. Ten States are still denied the representation in Congress to which they are entitled under the Constitution. It is this wrong which we have come here to protest against, and, as far as lies in us, to redress. [Great applause.] When the President of the United States declared that armed resistance to the authority of the Union was over, all the States had a right to be represented in the national legislature. [Loud cheering.] They had the right under the Constitution. They had the right under resolutions passed by both Houses of Congress in 1861. Those resolutions were not concurrent, but they were substantially identical. Moreover, the States were entitled to be so represented on other grounds of fairness and good faith. The President, not in pursuance of any Constitutional power, had called on the confederated States to accept certain conditions for their admission to the exercise of their legitimate functions as members of the Union—the ratification of the amendments to the Constitution abolishing slavery and the repudiation of the debts contracted to overthrow the Government. These conditions were met and accepted. The exaction of new conditions is unjust, a violation of the faith of the Government, subversive of the principles of our political system, and dangerous to the public prosperity and peace. [Applause.] Each House of Congress may, as the judge of the qualifications of its own members, reject individuals for just cause; but the two bodies, acting conjointly, cannot exclude entire delegations without an unwarrantable assumption of power. [Applause.] Congress has not only done this; it has gone farther. It has incorporated new conditions into amendments to the Constitution, and submitted them for the ratification of the States. There is no probability that these amendments will be ratified by three-fourths of the States. To insist on the conditions they contain is to prolong indefinitely the exclusion of more than one-fourth of the States from representation in Congress. [Applause.] Is this the Government our fathers fought to establish? [Cries of "No, no!"] Is this the Union we have been fighting to preserve? ["No, no!"] The President has done all in his power to correct this wrong [applause,] and to restore the legislative body to its full proportions, by giving all the members of the Union their proper share in the Public Councils. [Cheers.] Legislation without representation is an anomaly under our political system. Under any other form of government it would be but another name for usurpation and misrule. And the President is entitled to the thanks of the country for his firmness in opposing a policy so illiberal, so demoralizing, and so directly at war with every principle of our political organization.

I have referred to the condition of the legislative body under the aspects of right on the one hand and duty on the other—the right of the States to be represented and the duty of Congress to receive their representatives. On the score of policy, nothing can be more unwise than to prolong the present anomalous relation of the States to each other. It is calculated to embitter on both sides animosities and resentments which it is our duty, by all just measures, to sooth and heal. It disturbs the action of the Government; it deranges the application of capital and labor; it impedes the development of our resources; it impairs our credit and our good name at home and abroad; and it retards the march of the country to prosperity and power.

Gentlemen, I trust that in our deliberations here we shall confine ourselves to one main purpose—that of redressing the wrong to which I have referred. There is much in the administration of the Government which needs amendment—some things to be done, and others to be undone. There are commercial and financial reforms which are indispensable to the public welfare. But we shall not have the power to carry them out until we change the political complexion of Congress. [Enthusiastic and long continued applause.] This should be our first, our immediate aim. It is in the Congressional districts that the vital contest is to take place. The control of one branch of Congress will enable us to prevent partial, unjust, and pernicious legislation. The control of both Houses, with the power to introduce and carry out salutary reforms, to "bring the Government back," in the language of Jefferson, "to the republican tack," will come later. [Cheers.] But, with wise, harmonious, and judicious action on our part, and on the part of those we represent, this need not be long delayed. [Applause.] I believe that public opinion is right, and that it is only necessary to present to the people clearly the issues between us and the ultraism which controls the action of Congress. And, gentlemen, is not the object for which we are contending a consummation worthy of our highest and most devoted efforts?—to bring back the Republic, purified and strengthened by the fiery ordeal through which it has passed to its ancient prosperity and power [applause]—to present to the world an example worthy of imitation, not a mere Utopian vision of a good Government, but the grand old reality of the better times [applause] with which the memory of our fathers, the recollections of the past, and all our hopes of the future, are inseparably entwined [cheers]—*one country, one flag, one Union of equal States!* [Long continued applause.]

The remarks of General Dix were received with great enthusiasm. He was frequently interrupted by cheers. At the conclusion of his remarks the cheering was tremendous and long continued.

General Dix then said: It is proposed to open the proceedings of the Convention with ayer. He then introduced Rev. R. N. McDonald, who made the following prayer, the dience reverently standing:

THE OPENING PRAYER.

O Lord, high and mighty Ruler of the Universe, we, Thy dependent and needy crea-res, humbly draw near to Thee in the name of Thy beloved Son, our Lord and viour Jesus Christ. Have mercy on us according to Thy loving kindness; accord-g to the multitude of Thy tender mercies blot out our transgressions. We bless Thy ost high and holy name for the innumerable mercies Thou hast in Thy loving kind-ss bestowed on us as a Christian people. We bless Thee for the establishment and aintenance here of religious and civil liberty, and especially, O Lord, do we praise ee for the interposition of Thy power in our behalf in the late troubles which have en permitted to become upon our beloved country. We bless Thee that Thou hast ought to an end the fearful struggle in which the nation has been engaged, and that e Union has been preserved. Verily Thou art a God that doeth wonders. Thou ast make the wrath of man praise Thee, and Thou canst restrain the power thereof. e thank Thee that Thou hast put it in the hearts of Thy servants here present to semble from various parts of our land to consult for the public good; and now, O ost Mighty and Most Holy, let Thy blessing rest upon this Convention. May Thy rvants meet together as brothers and friends. Help them to lay aside all selfish otives, all unworthy personal and sectional considerations; enlighten their counsels; ide them in all their deliberations, so that the Union of the States may be fully stored and may be rendered perpetual. Restore their prosperity as at the first, and eir peace and fraternity as at the beginning. Bless the country in all its interests; its agriculture, in its commerce, and in the mechanical arts; in its churches, and its religious and benevolent institutions. Avert from us, we beseech Thee, the stilence that walketh in darkness, and the destruction that wasteth at noon-tide, and the judgments which our sins deserve. And, O most merciful God, our Heavenly ther, we beseech Thee to manifest Thine especial favor upon Thy servant, the esident of the United States. May his health and life be precious in Thy sight. ake him a great and lasting blessing to the country over which, in Thy wonderful d adorable providence, he has been called to bear rule. Bless his constitutional visers; gird him with wisdom and strength in every emergency. We pray, O rd, that he may be a just ruler in the fear of God, even as the light of the morning ien the sun ariseth—a morning without clouds—and as the tender grass springing m the earth after rain; and especially, O Lord, wilt Thou crown the efforts of Thy vant in maintaining the Union of these States inviolate under the Constitution tablished by our fathers. Bless all nations and their rulers. Let the Gospel be eached abroad. Thy kingdom come everywhere. Let oppression disappear among n. Let righteousness and peace reign over the whole earth. These are our peti-ns; these are our requests: O Lord, hear; O Lord, forgive; O Lord, hearken and l for his sake, our Great Redeemer, who hath taught us to say, Our Father who art Heaven, hallowed be Thy name; Thy kingdom come; Thy will be done on earth as s in Heaven. Give us this day our daily bread, and forgive us our trespasses as we give those that trespass against us. Lead us not into temptation, but deliver us m evil; for Thine is the kingdom, the power, and glory, forever. Amen.

During the delivery of the prayer the word amen was uttered frequently, with deep verence, in various parts of the house.

RESOLUTION TO APPOINT A COMMITTEE ON CREDENTIALS.

General Steedman. I have a resolution to offer providing for the appointment of a nmittee on the credentials of delegates to this Convention.

TEMPORARY SECRETARIES.

Hon. A. W. Randall. Before that resolution is put I beg leave to propose the follow-g appointments of temporary secretaries to the Convention: E. O. Perrin, of New rk; A. R. Potts, of Pennsylvania; John F. Coyle, of District of Columbia; James R. Beirne, of District of Columbia.

The Chairman. The call for this Convention will now be read:

THE CALL FOR THE CONVENTION.

A National Union Convention, of at least two delegates from each Congressional strict of all the States, two from each Territory, two from the District of Columbia, d four delegates at large from each State, will be held at the city of Philadelphia on e second Tuesday (14th) of August next.

Such delegates will be chosen by the electors of the several States who sustain the

Administration in maintaining unbroken the Union of the States under the Constitution which our fathers established, and who agree in the following propositions, viz.:

The Union of the States is, in every case, indissoluble, and is perpetual; and the Constitution of the United States, and the laws passed by Congress in pursuance thereof, supreme, and constant, and universal in their obligation;

The rights, the dignity, and the equality of the States in the Union, including the right of representation in Congress, are solemnly guaranteed by that Constitution, to save which from overthrow so much blood and treasure were expended in the late civil war;

There is no right, anywhere, to dissolve the Union, or to separate States from the Union, either by voluntary withdrawal, by force of arms, or by Congressional action; neither by the secession of the States, nor by the exclusion of their loyal and qualified representatives, nor by the National Government in any other form;

Slavery is abolished, and neither can, nor ought to be re-established in any State or Territory within our jurisdiction;

Each State has the undoubted right to prescribe the qualifications of its own electors, and no external power rightfully can, or ought to, dictate, control, or influence the free and voluntary action of the States in the exercise of that right;

The maintenance inviolate of the rights of the States, and especially of the right of each State to order and control its own domestic concerns, according to its own judgment exclusively, subject only to the Constitution of the United States, is essential to that balance of power on which the perfection and endurance of our political fabric depend, and the overthrow of that system by the usurpation and centralization of power in Congress would be a revolution, dangerous to republican government and destructive of liberty.

Each House of Congress is made, by the Constitution, the sole judge of the elections, returns, and qualifications of its members; but the exclusion of loyal Senators and Representatives, properly chosen and qualified under the Constitution and laws, is unjust and revolutionary.

Every patriot should frown upon all those acts and proceedings everywhere, which can serve no other purpose than to rekindle the animosities of war, and the effect of which upon our moral, social, and material interests at home, and upon our standing abroad, differing only in degree, is injurious like war itself.

The purpose of the war having been to preserve the Union and Constitution by putting down the rebellion, and the rebellion having been suppressed, all resistance to the authority of the General Government being at an end, and the war having ceased, war measures should also cease, and should be followed by measures of peaceful administration, so that union, harmony, and concord may be encouraged, and industry, commerce, and the arts of peace revived and promoted; and the early restoration of all the States to the exercise of their constitutional powers in the National Government is indispensably necessary to the strength and the defence of the Republic, and to the maintenance of the public credit.

All such electors in the thirty-six States and nine Territories of the United States, and in the District of Columbia, who, in a spirit of patriotism and love for the Union, can rise above personal and sectional considerations, and who desire to see a truly National Union Convention, which shall represent all the States and Territories of the Union, assemble, as friends and brothers, under the national flag, to hold counsel together upon the state of the Union, and to take measures to avert possible danger from the same, are specially requested to take part in the choice of such delegates.

But no delegate will take a seat in such Convention who does not loyally accept the national situation and cordially endorse the principles above set forth, and who is not attached, in true allegiance, to the Constitution, the Union, and the Government of the United States.

WASHINGTON, *June* 25, 1866.

A. W. RANDALL, *President.*
J. R. DOOLITTLE,
O. H. BROWNING,
EDGAR COWAN,
CHARLES KNAP,
SAMUEL FOWLER,
Executive Committee National Union Club.

We recommend the holding of the above Convention, and endorse the call therefor.

DANIEL S. NORTON,
J. W. NESMITH,
JAMES DIXON,
T. A. HENDRICKS.

ORDER OF BUSINESS.

Hon. J. R. DOOLITTLE.—With the leave of the gentleman from Ohio, and before the otion is put on his resolution to appoint a committee on credentials, I ask leave to bmit two resolutions, which have reference to the order of business in this Conven- m. The first resolution which I offer, with his leave, will be this:

Resolved, That, until otherwise ordered, the general rules of the House of Representives of the United States, so far as applicable, govern the proceedings of this Con- ntion, and, until otherwise ordered, in case any question shall arise to be determined r a division, or by the ayes and noes, the Secretary shall call the roll of all the ates and Territories of the United States and the District of Columbia. Each State, called, shall be entitled to cast double the number of votes to which it is entitled in e electoral college, as its delegation shall direct; and each Territory, and also the istrict of Columbia, shall be entitled to cast two votes, as their several delegations all direct.

The resolution was unanimously adopted.

Hon. J. R. DOOLITTLE.—I desire also to submit the following resolution:

Resolved, That all resolutions and propositions not relating to the organization of the onvention, be referred by the Chair to the Committee on Resolutions, hereafter to be ppointed, without debate; and that all resolutions, propositions, and questions relang to the right or claim of any person to a seat in the Convention, be referred by e Chair to the Committee on Credentials, hereaftor to be appointed, without debate; nd that until the appointment of such committee they do lie upon the table, without ebate.

This resolution was unanimously agreed to.

The Secretary then read the resolution offered by General Steedman, as follows:

Resolved, That a committee of thirteen be appointed by the Chair as a committee on redentials.

This resolution was unanimously adopted.

PERMANENT ORGANIZATION.

Hon. MONTGOMERY BLAIR.—I wish to offer the following resolution, providing for the ermanent organization of this Convention:

Resolved, That a committee of one from each State be appointed by the Chair to re- ort officers for the permanent organization of the Convention.

Hon. THOMAS B. FLORENCE.—It strikes me, sir, inasmuch as there is great misappre- ension as to the character of the delegations to this body, that the Secretary be equested to read the circular issued over the signature of Judge Blair and others, nown as the "Blair-Campbell Circular," inviting the coöperation of Democrats, as uch, in this body. It seems to me that if there was any significance in reading the riginal call, the supplementary call is quite as important to remove any misappre- ension that may occur as to the position we may occupy. I suggest that it be read.

THE CHAIRMAN.—If there is no objection, it will be read.

It was then read, as follows:

THE CONGRESSIONAL ADDRESS.

To the People of the United States:

Dangers threaten. The Constitution—the citadel of our liberties—is directly assailed. The future is dark, unless the people will come to the rescue.

In this hour of peril National Union should be the watchword of every true man.

As essential to National Union, we must maintain unimpaired the rights, the dignity, and the equality of the States, including the right of representation in Congress, and the exclusive right of each State to control its own domestic concerns, subject only to the Constitution of the United States.

After a uniform construction of the Constitution for more than half a century, the assumption of new and arbitrary powers in the Federal Government is subversive of our system and destructive of liberty.

A free interchange of opinion and kind feeling between the citizens of all the States is necessary to the perpetuity of the Union. At present eleven States are excluded from the National Council. For seven long months the present Congress has persistently denied any right of representation to the people of these States. Laws, affecting their highest and dearest interests, have been passed without their consent, and in disregard of the fundamental principle of free Government. This denial of representation has been made to all the members from a State, although the State, in the language of the President, "presents itself, not only in an attitude of loyalty and harmony, but in the persons of representatives whose loyalty cannot be questioned under any existing constitutional or legal test." The representatives of nearly one-third of the States have not been consulted with reference to the great questions of the day. There has been no nationality surrounding the present Congress. There has been no intercourse between the representatives of the two sections, producing mutual confidence and respect. In the language of the distinguished Lieutenant-General, "It is to be regretted that, at this time, there cannot be a greater commingling between the citizens of the two sections, and particularly those entrusted with the law-making power." This state of things should be removed at once and forever.

Therefore, to preserve the National Union, to vindicate the supremacy of our admirable Constitution, to guard the States from covert attempts to deprive them of their true position in the Union, and bring together those who are unnaturally severed, and for these great national purposes only, we cordially approve the call for a National Union Convention, to be held at the city of Philadelphia, on the second Tuesday (14th) of August next, and endorse the principles therein set forth.

We, therefore, respectfully, but earnestly, urge upon our fellow-citizens in each State, and Territory, and Congressional District of the United States, in the interest of Union and in a spirit of harmony, and with direct reference to the principles contained in said call, to act promptly in the selection of wise, moderate, and conservative men to represent them in said Convention, to the end that *all* States shall at once be restored to their practical relations to the Union, the Constitution maintained, and peace bless the whole country.

W. E. Niblack,	Reverdy Johnson,
Anthony Thornton,	Thomas A. Hendricks,
Michael C. Kerr,	Wm. Wright,
G. S. Shanklin,	James Guthrie,
Garrett Davis,	J. A. McDougall,
H. Grider,	Wm. Radford,
Thomas E. Noell,	S. S. Marshall,
Sam'l J. Randall,	Myer Strouse,
Lewis W. Ross,	Chas. Sitgreaves,
Stephen Tabor,	S. E. Ancona,
J. M. Humphreys,	E. N. Hubbell,
John Hogan,	B. C. Ritter,
B. M. Boyer,	A. Harding,
Tennis G. Bergen,	A. J. Glossbrenner,
Chas. Goodyear,	E. R. V. Wright,
Chas. H. Winfield,	A. J. Rogers,
A. H. Coffroth,	H. McCullough,
Lovell H. Rousseau,	F. C. Le Blond,
Philip Johnson,	W. E. Finck,
Chas. A. Eldridge,	L. S. Trimble.
John L. Dawson,	

WASHINGTON, July 4, 1866.

Col. THOMAS B. FLORENCE. I have no objection to that, but it is not the one I referred to. I mean the circular issued over the signatures of Governor Randall and Judge Blair.

THE CHAIRMAN. It is not in the possession of the Secretary.

Mr. FLORENCE, (handing a paper to the Secretary.) That is the paper to which I allude. That is a very patriotic paper, and there can be no earthly objection to reading it; and I ask, that after reading the other, the Secretary may also read this which I have presented. A paper which has met the response of so many persons here, and has met with such universal approval, cannot do any harm to this Convention.

The circular presented by Mr. Florence was then read by the Secretary as follows:

SUPPLEMENTARY CIRCULAR.

WASHINGTON, D. C., July 10, 1866.

Your immediate and earnest attention is invited to the annexed call for a National Convention, issued by the National Union Executive Committee, and the accompanying endorsement thereof by prominent gentlemen who are well known to the country.

The undersigned have been duly appointed a committee to facilitate and expedite, by correspondence and otherwise, such action as may seem necessary to bring together at Philadelphia a convention of the ablest men of the nation, without regard to their party antecedents, who favor, generally, the restoration policy President Johnson has advocated against the dangerous course pursued by the majority of Congress.

We deem it proper to suggest that it is desirable that there be sent from each State four delegates at large and two from each Congressional district who favor the principles set forth in the call, to be taken from the supporters of Lincoln and Johnson in 1864, and a like number from their opponents. Also, four delegates from each Territory, and four from the District of Columbia. In those States whereof a portion of the people were lately in rebellion, a corresponding number of delegates may be chosen by the people generally, who accept the principles stated in the call. It is not intended, however, that these suggestions shall interfere with any arrangements already made for the selection of delegates. It is left entirely to the political organizations in the different States and districts that occur in the principles of the call to decide whether they will choose their delegates by joint or separate meetings, or by their executive committees.

We have been authorized to appoint temporary executive committees in the States where the same are presumed to be necessary. You are, therefore, requested to act as such committee, and to adopt immediate measures to secure a full delegation to the proposed Convention, not interfering, however, with the action which existing organizations may have taken for the same object. Your action will be such as to aid such movements—the purpose of your appointment being to provide for the selection of delegates if no adequate preliminary arrangements have yet been made.

The day fixed for the National Convention is near, and we desire to impress on you and all friends of this cause, that it is of the first importance that District or State Conventions, or State Executive Committees, immediately appoint delegates. And it is particularly requested that a list of delegates and committees appointed be speedily forwarded to the Chairman of this Committee.

In conclusion, we have to add that the paramount object of this movement is to bring into a great National Conference from all parts of our distracted country wise and patriotic men, who may devise a plan of political action calculated to restore national unity, fraternity, and harmony, and secure to an afflicted people that which is so sincerely desired by all good men—the practical blessings of an enduring peace.

ALEX. W. RANDALL,
LEWIS D. CAMPBELL,
MONTGOMERY BLAIR.

The Secretary then read the appointments made on the Committees on Credentials and on Organization. They are as follows:

COMMITTEE ON CREDENTIALS.

JAMES B. STEEDMAN, Ohio, Chairman; N. D. Coleman, Louisiana; Thomas Hoyne, Illinois; Charles P. Daly, New York; David Kilgore, Indiana; J. B. Campbell, South Carolina; A. Hyatt Smith, Wisconsin; Geo. M. Ives, Connecticut; B. H. Epperson, Texas; E. W. Pierce, Massachusetts; Ashbel Green, New Jersey; James McFerren, Missouri; John R. Franklin, Maryland.

COMMITTEE ON ORGANIZATION

Hon. MONTGOMERY BLAIR, Maryland, Chairman; Nathaniel S. Little, Maine; E. A. Hibbard, New Hampshire; J. J. Deavitt, Vermont; E. A. Alger, Massachusetts; A. Ballou, Rhode Island; Loren P. Waldo, Connecticut; Hon. W. H. Ludlow, New York; Hon. Joel Parker, New Jersey; Hon. H. W. Tracy, Pennsylvania; Joseph M. Barr, Delaware; Thomas S. Flournoy, Virginia; John J. Thompson, West Virginia; W. A. Wright, North Carolina; T. N. Dawkins, South Carolina; Porter Ingram, Florida; James B. Dawkins, Georgia, Hon. J. F. Bailey, Mississippi; J. G. Parham, Louisiana; J. B. Luce, Arkansas; B. H. Epperson, Texas; Jos. Ramsay, Tennessee; Alexander White, Alabama; Hon. E. A. Graves, Kentucky; George Fries, Ohio; Colonel D. G. Rose, Indiana; Hon. Thomas J. Turner, Illinois; General A. A. Stephens, Michigan; Robert Wilson, Missouri; H. M. Rice, Minnesota; L. B. Vilas, Wisconsin; J. H. Murphy, Iowa; Nicholas Smith, Kansas; Hon. Samuel Purdy, California; G. M. Beebe, Nevada; W. H. Farrar, Oregon; Owen Thorn, District of Columbia; ——— ———, Arizona; A. J. Faulk, Dakota; Thomas W. Betts, Idaho, ——— ———, Montana; Hon. J. Sterling Morton, Nebraska; Geo. P. Este, New Mexico; ——— ———, Utah; ——— ———, Colorado; Elwood Evans, Washington Territory.

THE CHAIRMAN. The list of the members of this Committee has been read by States.

It is understood that Mr. Blair, of Maryland, is Chairman of the Committee on Organization.

ADJOURNMENT.

Hon. MONTGOMERY BLAIR. I move that this Convention now adjourn till to-morrow at twelve o'clock.

The Convention thereupon was adjourned.

SECOND DAY.

The Convention met at 12 o'clock M., pursuant to adjournment.

THE CHAIRMAN. The Convention will come to order, and gentlemen will pleas take their seats.

The Rev. John P. Haltzinger, of Greenville, Tennessee, then offered the openin prayer:

THE PRAYER.

Almighty God, our Heavenly Father, "Thou hast been our dwelling place in a generations, before ever Thou hadst formed the earth and the world, even from eve lasting to everlasting. Thou art God." We desire to approach Thee in the name c Thy Son Jesus Christ, and ask Thee for His sake to pardon all our sins, and forgive al our iniquities. In Thy Providence we have been brought together at this place for special purpose; and we ask Thee, Almighty Father, to give us a suitable spirit fo the present occasion, and help us to feel the responsibility resting upon us. As mil lions are to be affected by this great meeting, for weal or woe, please guide this Con vention in wisdom, that good may result from all its counsels. We would most de voutly thank Thee for all Thy mercies; and as the storms of war are past, grant u peace and unity in all the borders of our beloved country, that there may be perfec harmony in the great arch of States represented on this occasion; that the constella tion of thirty-six stars seen in the blue field of our national emblem may never b diminished. May our Union be permanent; may it last through all time. We ask that it may *still be the Union of our Fathers;* and may their mantle fall upon us, and may we who are here have the spirit of '76. We ask Thee for temporal blessings. May our fields produce, and may our flocks increase, and our substance multiply; and may all be spent to Thy glory. We pray for our rulers, and ask that they may be men fearing God, and hating covetousness. And most especially do we pray Thy blessing upon the President of the United States. Grant him the head, the heart, and the hands competent to his great task; and may the nation prosper under his administration. In a very few years we will be called to sleep the long sleep of death—to render an account of all our acts. May we so live that our conduct in life will be for the glory of God and good of our race; and when a dying hour comes, may we be at peace with all our fellow-men, and in favor with God. And, finally, through the blood of our blessed Redeemer, we hope to praise the name of God, the Father, Son, and Spirit, in a world without end. Amen.

REPORTS OF COMMITTEES.

THE CHAIRMAN. The first business before the Convention is the report of committees.

Hon. MONTGOMERY BLAIR. I am instructed by the Committee on Organization to make the following report of the officers of the Convention.

THE CHAIRMAN. The Secretary will read the report from the Committee on Organization.

THE SECRETARY. The report of the Committee on Organization is as follows:

REPORT OF COMMITTEE ON ORGANIZATION.

For President.—Hon. JAMES R. DOOLITTLE, of Wisconsin.

For Vice Presidents.—Leonard Wood, LL.D., Maine; Daniel Marcy, New Hampshire; Myron Clark, Vermont; Hon. R. B. Hall, Massachusetts; Alfred Anthony, Rhode Island; Hon. O. F. Winchester, Connecticut; Hon. Theodore S. Faxton, New York; Gen. Gershom Mott, New Jersey; Asa Packer, Pennsylvania; Ayres Stockley, Delaware; Gen. George Vickers, Maryland; Hon. John W. Brockenborough, Virginia; Thomas Sweeney, West Virginia; Hon. John A. Gilmer, North Carolina; Judge David Lewis Wardlaw, South Carolina; Richard S. Lyons, Georgia; Judge Thomas Randall, Florida; G. A. Sykes, Mississippi; Cuthbert Bullitt, Louisiana; J. M. Tebbetts, Arkansas; D. J. Burnett, Texas; Thomas A. R. Nelson, Tennessee; George S. Houston, Alabama; Hon. J. W. Ritter, Kentucky; Hon. P. Ranney, Ohio; Hon. W. S. Smith, Indiana; D. K. Green, Illinois; Hon. O. B. Clark, Michigan; Hon. John Hogan, Missouri; Franklin Steele, Minnesota; Gen. Milton Montgomery, Wisconsin; Edward Johnston, Iowa; J. L. Pendery, Kansas; William T. Coleman, California; Frank Hereford, Nevada; Hon. George L. Curry, Oregon; Joseph H. Bradley, Sr., District of Columbia; ——— ———, Arizona; J. W. Turner, Dakota; Charles F. Powell, Idaho; George L. Miller, Nebraska; ——— ———, New Mexico; ——— ———, Utah; Hon. B. F. Hall, Colorado; Elwood Evans, Washington Territory.

For Secretaries.—James Mann, Maine; E. S. Cutter, New Hampshire; George H. Simmons, Vermont; Charles Wright, Massachusetts; James H. Parsons, Rhode Island; James A. Hovey, Connecticut; E. O. Perrin, New York; Col. Thomas S. Allison, New Jersey; Harry A. Weaver, Pennsylvania; J. F. Tharp, Delaware; Dr. W. W. Watns, Maryland; Thomas Wallace, Virginia; Henry S. Walker, West Virginia; F. Patterson, North Carolina; Thomas Y. Simmons, South Carolina; J. H. Christie, orgia; Judge B. D. Wright, Florida; A. G. Mayer, Mississippi; A. W. Walker, uisiana; Elias C. Boudinot, Arkansas; J. M. Daniel, Texas; John Lellyet, Tenssee; C. S. G. Doster, Alabama; M. H. Owsley, Kentucky; E. B. Eshelman, Ohio; l. C. C. Matson, Indiana; John McGinnis, Jr., Illinois; Gen. John G. Parkhurst, ichigan; Col. C. B. Wilkinson, Missouri; Richard Price, Minnesota; George C. nty, Wisconsin; J. M. Walker, Iowa; W. A. Tipton, Kansas; Jackson Temple, Calirnia; Col. Jesse Williams, Nevada; A. D. Fitch, Oregon; James R. O'Beirne, Disct of Columbia; D. T. Bramble, Dakota; Major L. Lowrie, Nebraska; Charles P. an, Washington.

The Chairman, GENERAL DIX, at this point introduced the Senator from Wisconsin, 10, upon stepping to the front of the platform, was received with immense cheers— e whole assemblage rising as one man, and the applause continued until order was lled. Senator DOOLITTLE then said:

MR. DOOLITTLE'S SPEECH.

Gentlemen of the Convention and Fellow-Citizens of the United States: [Cheers.] For e distinguished honor of being called upon to preside over the deliberations of this nvention, I sincerely thank you. I could have wished that its responsibilities had len upon another, but relying upon that courtesy and generous confidence which has lled me to the chair, I enter at once upon its duties with an earnest desire for the ccess of the great cause in which we are now engaged. Among the great events of r own day this Convention, in my opinion, will prove to be one of the greatest, for peace hath her victories not less renowned than war." [Applause.] And this Conven-n is one of her victories—may I not say a crowning victory? [Applause.] For the st time in six years a National Convention representing all the States is now assem-ed. [Applause.] Six long, weary years! As we look back, oh! what an interval blood, and agony, and tears! During that period we have been engaged in the most gantic civil war the world has ever seen, wasting our resources, drenching a thousand ttle-fields with fraternal blood, and carrying to a premature grave our fathers, our ns, and our brothers by hundreds of thousands.

But, thanks be to Almighty God, the war is over, [enthusiastic cheering and apause,] and what we here witness assures us that peace has come, and come to stay. pplause.] Fellow-citizens, if the people of the United States could at this moment k in upon this Convention, if they could see what we now witness, the North and South, the East and the West, joining together in fraternal association as friends d fellow-citizens, our work would be already done. [Cheering and applause.] If ey could have seen—as we saw—Massachusetts and South Carolina, [applause,] by eir full delegations, coming arm in arm [applause] into this great Convention, pplause;] if they could have seen this body, greater in numbers, and in weight of aracter and brain, than ever yet assembled on this Continent under one roof, pplause,] melting to tears of joy and gratitude to witness this commingling, there uld be no struggle at the polls in the coming elections. [Applause.]

When I remember that it was Massachusetts and South Carolina that, in the Conntion which framed the Constitution, voted against the abolition of the slave de; that it was Massachusetts in 1812 which, through some of her men, taught heresy of nullification, which South Carolina reasserted in 1832, and in the form of ession again in 1860; when I call to mind that South Carolina fired the first n, and that the veins of Massachusetts poured out the first blood in the recent uggle; and when I call to mind all these memories, and at the same time see these o old States of the Union coming here in fraternal embrace, approaching a common ar of a common country, ready to make sacrifices for the good of the whole—I say ain, could the whole people of the United States witness all this, there would remain further work for us to restore the Union. [Applause.] If the people of Massachuts herself could have witnessed it, not a single member could be returned to Conss [enthusiastic cheering and applause] from that State until he had given the st sacred pledge that he would do all in his power in Congress to recognize the ality and dignity of all States under the Constitution, [applause and cheering,] luding the sacred, inalienable right of every State under the Constitution to repretation in both Houses. [Cheering and applause.] Gentlemen of the Convention, hall go into no argument on this occasion. [A voice, "Go on, go on."] The disguished gentleman who preceded me said all that I now desire to say, and much ter than I could say it. [Voice, "Go on."] I endorse, and take great pleasure in ly endorsing, all that he said—sentence by sentence and word by word. [Applause.] Fellow-citizens, unfortunately the whole people of the Northern States do not ness what is now transpiring here; therefore, the greater work still rests upon us from this time until the election of the next Congress. We should be untiring in our exertions to see to it that if this Congress shall continue to refuse this sacred right of representation to equal States, that the next Congress shall recognize them. [Cheers and applause.] When that is done, the Union is restored. [Applause.] And when the Union is restored, we shall be prepared, in my judgment, to enter upon a higher and nobler career among the nations of the earth than has yet been occupied by any Government upon which the sun of Heaven ever shone. [Applause.] We shall stand in the vanguard of civilization, of liberty; we shall lead by the light of our example all other nations of the earth.

Gentlemen, without detaining you longer, I shall enter at once upon the duties of the chair. [Enthusiastic and prolonged cheering and applause.]

The band here struck up the inspiring notes of the Star-Spangled Banner.

THE PRESIDENT. The gentlemen who have been chosen as vice presidents of the Convention will now please to come forward and take their seats upon the platform to the right and to the left of the Chair, and while they are so doing the music will continue.

Here the band struck up the popular air "Tramp, Tramp," until the vice presidents and secretaries had assumed their places.

THE PRESIDENT. The Convention will now be in order.

GENERAL STEEDMAN. I have leave to present the report of the Committee on Credentials, which I now hand to the Chair.

THE PRESIDENT. The gentleman from Ohio offers the following report from the Committee on Credentials. The Secretary will read the report.

THE SECRETARY. The following report is made by the chairman of the Committee on Credentials:

REPORT OF THE COMMITTEE ON CREDENTIALS.

The Committee on Credentials report that they have considered the credentials of all the delegates presented to them, and that in no State has any contest occurred except in Maine, Delaware, and New York, and in these cases they have made the following disposition:

The delegation elected by the meeting held at Rutland, headed by Governor Crosby, in the opinion of the Committee, are entitled to admission as delegates from the State of Maine.

The Committee recommend that the delegation from Delaware, elected by the meeting held at Dover, on the 26th of July, be admitted as delegates from that State. The Committee recommend that the persons chosen by the meeting held at Wilmington, on the 2d of August, be admitted to honorary seats in this Convention.

They also recommend that the gentlemen attending from the New York Service Society of Soldiers and Sailors, and the gentlemen recommended by the chairman of the New York delegation, be admitted to seats as honorary members, and that, inasmuch as the reading of the list of the delegates must occupy much time, the Committee recommend the reading be dispensed with, and that the list be published with the proceedings of the Convention.

GENERAL STEEDMAN. For the information of the Convention I will state that room 44 at the Continental Hotel is the headquarters of the Committee on Credentials. A book containing the names of all the delegates is on the table of the Secretary of this Convention, and will be taken to that room when the Convention adjourns, for the purpose of adding the names of such delegates as have reported since this report was made up. To enable the Convention to proceed to the consideration of business for which it has been assembled, I now move the previous question on the adoption of the report of the Committee.

THE PRESIDENT. The question is upon the adoption of the report of the committee. Those who are in favor of its adoption will signify the same by saying "aye."

The report was unanimously adopted.

VALLANDIGHAM'S WITHDRAWAL.

Hon. W. S. GROESBECK, of Ohio. I desire to present a letter from a gentleman who was elected a delegate to this Convention, but who has declined to take his place as such. The letter is from the Hon. C. L. Vallandigham. I would further state that I present this as the organ of the united delegations of the State of Ohio, and it being addressed to the Convention, I desire it may be read.

THE PRESIDENT. The gentleman presents a letter from the Hon. C. L. Vallandigham, and desires the same shall be read. [Cheers from portions of the hall.] It requires the unanimous consent of the Convention.

Mr. HUGH L. GARDNER, of New York, and others. I object.

Hon. REVERDY JOHNSON, of Maryland. If it be a fact that it requires the unanimous consent of the Convention, I move the rules be suspended.

Hon. LEWIS D. CAMPBELL, of Ohio. I second the motion.

The question was then put on the suspension of the rules, and the motion to suspend was agreed to.

THE PRESIDENT. The Secretary will now read the letter from the Hon. C. L. Vallandigham. [Cheering.]

THE SECRETARY. The letter is as follows:

VALLANDIGHAM'S LETTER.

GIRARD HOUSE, PHILADELPHIA, August 14, 1866.

To the Chairman of the National Union Convention:

SIR: I have this day received from the National Union Committee, through the Hon. William S. Groesbeck, chairman of the joint Ohio delegation to your Convention, a ticket of admission as a delegate from that State.

Hon. George W. McCook, chairman of the Democratic delegation from Ohio, has also communicated to me the following resolution, adopted this morning by the delegation:

Resolved unanimously by the Ohio delegation, That we recognize the right of Clement L. Vallandigham, a duly elected delegate from the Third Congressional District of Ohio, to hold a seat in that Convention. That we should regard his exclusion from such seat as an unjust and unreasonable infringement of the rights of the Democracy of said district, and are ready to stand by him in the assertion of his rights and the rights of his constituents; and that we endorse cordially the purity and patriotism of his motives and his fitness every way to sit in said Convention Yet, for the sake of harmony and good feeling in the same, and in order to secure the great ends for which it is called, we consent to his withdrawal from this delegation and from a seat in this Convention, if, in his judgment, his duty to his constituents shall justify such withdrawal.

Yielding my own deliberate convictions of duty and right to the almost unanimous opinion and desire of friends, whose wisdom, soundness of judgment, and sincerity and purity of motives I may not question, to the end that there shall be no pretext even from any quarter for any controverted question or disturbing element in the Convention to mar its harmony, or to hinder in any way the good results to the cause of the Convention, the Union, and the public liberty, which shall follow from its deliberations and its actions, I hereby withdraw from the Ohio Democratic delegation, and decline taking my seat in the Convention. I am profoundly conscious that the sanctity and magnitude of the interests involved in the present political canvass in the United States are too immense not to demand a sacrifice of every personal consideration in a struggle upon the issue of which depends, as I solemnly believe, the present peace, and ultimately the existence of free republican government on this continent.

Trusting that your deliberations may be harmonious, your proceedings full of the spirit of wisdom and patriotism, and its results crowned with a glorious and saving triumph in the end to the great cause in which every sympathy of my heart is enlisted, am, very respectfully, &c., C. L. VALLANDIGHAM.

ENTHUSIASTIC RECEPTION OF HON. EDGAR COWAN.

Hon. EDGAR COWAN. You——[The cheering that arose when the Senator was seen standing continued for some minutes. The ladies joined in it, and hats and handkerchiefs were waved, till the whole large mass seemed like one huge wave agitated by a passing wind. The tall form of the Senator turned towards them, and he seemed perfectly overwhelmed at this spontaneous exhibition of his national popularity. The cheering subsided once or twice, and was renewed again and again. At last he said:]

You will excuse me for this time; I only beg leave to offer the following resolution, which I will send to the Chair.

THE PRESIDENT. The resolution will be read.

THE SECRETARY. The resolution is as follows:

RESOLUTION FOR A COMMITTEE ON ADDRESS AND RESOLUTIONS.

Resolved, That a committee of two from each State and Territory be appointed to prepare resolutions and an address for the Convention.

The resolution passed unanimously.

THE PRESIDENT. The following despatch has just been received from the President of the United States. [Long and enthusiastic cheering.]

THE SECRETARY. I will now read the despatch:

DESPATCH FROM THE PRESIDENT.

WASHINGTON, August 14, 1866.

To the Hon. O. H. Browning and A. W. Randall, Convention at Philadelphia:

I thank you for your cheering and encouraging despatch. The finger of Providence is unerring, and will guide you safely through. The people must be trusted, and the country will be restored. My faith is unshaken as to the ultimate success.

ANDREW JOHNSON.

[Great cheers.]

The President. The Chair will now announce the names of the Committee on Res lutions and Address. There are some States for which names have not been present to the Chair, and when the names have been read of those who have been appoint the Chair will have the names of those States called in order, and the delegations fro those States can send the names of two persons from each State to the Committee Resolutions, and their names will be inserted. The Secretary will now read the nam of the committee.

The Secretary. The names are as follows:

[The Secretary then read the list of names.]

Hon. O. H. Browning, of Illinois. Mr. President, the names as announced conta that of Charles L. Woodbury in lieu of that of S. S. Marvin. I ask to have the latt inserted.

The President. It will be inserted.

Mr. Lawrence. The name of Thomas Steers is omitted. I ask that it be inserted.

The President. It will be inserted.

Mr. B. Able, of Missouri. The names from Missouri were omitted. I ask that the of Governor Austin A. King and James O. Broadhead be inserted from Missouri.

The President. Those names will be inserted. The corrected list will now be rea

The Secretary. The corrected list is as follows:

COMMITTEE ON RESOLUTIONS AND ADDRESS.

Hon. Edgar Cowan, Chairman; Maine, R. D. Rice, George M. Weston; New Ham shire, C. B. Bowers, H. Bingham; Vermont, C. N. Davenport, J. H. Williams; M sachusetts, General D. N. Couch, C. L. Woodbury; Rhode Island, William Bea Lawrence, Thomas Steere; Connecticut, James Dixon, Origen S. Seymour; New Yo Hon. Henry J. Raymond, Hon. Sanford E. Church; New Jersey, Colonel Ingh Coriell, Abraham Browning; Pennsylvania, Hon. Edgar Cowan, Hon. William Bigle Delaware, Joseph P. Comeygs, Ayres Stockley; Maryland, Hon. Reverdy Johnson, H John W. Crisfield; West Virginia, General John J. Jackson, Daniel Lamb; Virgin Hon. Richard H. Parker, John L. Marye; North Carolina, Hon. William A. Graha Hon. Nathaniel Boyden; South Carolina, S. McGowan, B. F. Perry; Georgia, P. Alexander, A. R. Wright; Florida, Hon. William Marvin, Hon. Wilkinson Call; A bama, C. C. Langdon, T. J. Foster; Mississippi, William Yerger, Hon. A. Murdoc Louisiana, Hon. John Ray, Joshua Baker; Texas, B. H. Epperson, L. D. Eva Tennessee, Hon. John S. Brien, Hon. John Baxter; Arkansas, William Byers, M. Bell; Kentucky, Hon. E. Hise, Hon. Garrett Davis; Ohio, Solomon Hinckle, Gene George W. McCook; Indiana, John S. Davis, Hon. Thomas A. Hendricks; Ilin Hon. O. H. Browning, Hon. S. S. Marshall; Michigan, William B. McCreary, H Charles E. Stewart; Missouri, Austin A. King, James O. Broadhead; Minnesota, He M. Rice, Daniel S. Norton; Wisconsin, C. A. Eldridge, J. J. R. Pease; Iowa, Char Mason, Thomas H. Benton, jr.; Kansas, General Charles W. Blair, W. C. McDowe California, R. J. Walker, J. A. McDougall; Nevada, Governor G. M. Beebe, Fra Hereford; Oregon, G. L. Curry, E. M. Barnum; District of Columbia, Richard Merrick, Dr. Charles Allen; Arizona, ———; Dakota, A. J. Faulk; Idaho, C. Powell, Henry W. Pugh; Montana, ———; Nebraska, General H. H. Heath; N Mexico, George P. Este; Utah, ———; Washington, Edward Lander; Colora Milo Lee.

The President. The committee will now retire for purposes of consultation into committee room, on the left of the Chair.

General Carroll, of New York. I offer the following resolution:

REVISION OF OUR NEUTRALITY LAWS.

Resolved, That there is demanded a revision of our national neutrality laws, in c sequence of the spirit of the age, and that it was the duty of Congress to com with the public demand for the revision of the same.

This resolution was referred to the Committee on Resolutions.

Mr. S. S. Hayes, of Illinois. I move the adoption of the following resolution u the order of business——

The President. The gentleman will wait a moment until the Committee on Res tions have an opportunity to retire.

Mr. S. S. Hayes, of Illinois, offers the following resolution, which will be read.

The Secretary then read the resolution, as follows:

INSTRUCTIONS TO THE COMMITTEE ON RESOLUTIONS.

Resolved, That the Committee on Resolutions be authorized and directed to rep in print, and to supply each member of the Convention with a copy of the resoluti reported, at the time of their presentation.

Mr. APGAR, of New York. Do I understand that it is expected that the Chairman of the Committee will not report directly to the Convention?

THE PRESIDENT. The resolution will again be read.

The Secretary re-read the resolution.

Mr. APGAR, of New York. I apprehend that under the resolution adopted for your Convention as a rule of its proceedings, this resolution must go to the Committee on Resolutions without debate.

THE PRESIDENT. I think the point taken by the gentleman from New York is correct. This resolution will go to the Committe on Resolutions under the rule already adopted. [Slight applause.]

REMARKS OF MR. HAYES, OF ILLINOIS.

Mr. HAYES, of Illinois. I rise to a point of order. I understand by the remarks of the gentleman from New York that the resolutions, under the rule, must go to the Committee on Resolutions without the action of this Convention, and upon that motion or suggestion I am prepared to say one single word.

I was asked the object of the resolution, and in answer would say, that I understand by the rule of proceedings adopted by the Convention that all resolutions containing a declaration of principle, or having reference to the platform adopted by this Convention, shall go before the Convention through a committee appointed to consider the effect of those resolutions. But the resolution proposed by me is not a resolution in relation to principle, or in relation to the general action of this Convention. It is simply a direction to the Committee on Resolutions to make a report in such a manner that this Convention may be fully posted on the subject of the resolutions before it acts upon them. Sir, I came to this Convention with a sincere, a disinterested purpose. I came here with no personal object to attain, so far as I know, so help me God. Sir, I am a member of what is called the Democratic party of this country, [applause,] and, sir, I came here with the utmost enthusiasm for the great cause in which we are all united. Sir, I expect that this Convention will do or say nothing in the platform to which I, as a consistent and Union-loving Democrat, cannot heartily subscribe. [Applause.] I know the Democratic party of this country. I, sir, am proud to be a member of that party, and I believe that if there ever was a patriotic party in the world it is the Democratic party of this country. [Applause.] I desire to say—[Voices, "Question," "question," "question."]

Mr. APGAR, of New York. I rise to a point of order.

Mr. HAYES, of Illinois. One word more.

THE PRESIDENT. The gentleman from Illinois will allow the Chair to state that there is a gentleman rising on the left to a point of order. It may have escaped his attention. There is no question before the Convention, as no appeal was taken from the decision of the Chair.

Mr. HAYES, of Illinois. I don't propose to dissent from the action of the Convention, although it was taken without argument, on the decision of the Chair. I had merely one word of explanation. I believe that that resolution, in the form in which it appears to the committee, will meet with their careful consideration; but I wish to add, as a reason for introducing it now, that the resolutions shall be carefully considered by the delegations, and be in print, so that each delegation shall meet together and unanimously adopt them. [Applause.]

Mr. APGAR, of New York. The gentleman is out of order.

THE PRESIDENT. There is no question before the House, and the gentleman has taken his seat.

Mr. HOGAN, of Missouri. I move that this Convention take a recess for an hour or two, to allow the committee to deliberate upon the resolutions.

[Voices, "No," "no," "no."]

THE PRESIDENT. The gentleman from Missouri suggests that the Convention take a recess of two hours.

[The name of Milo Lee was here inserted on the Committee on Resolutions and adopted.]

Mr. COWAN, of Pennsylvania. I beg leave to report that the committee have not organized, and will not be able to report finally to the Convention before to-morrow at ten o'clock, and therefore ask leave to sit until that time.

THE PRESIDENT. It is moved that when this Convention adjourns it adjourn to meet again to-morrow morning at ten o'clock.

A motion was then made as an amendment to the previous motion, that when the Convention adjourns it adjourn to meet to-morrow at twelve o'clock.

THE PRESIDENT. It is moved and seconded that when this Convention adjourns it adjourn to meet to-morrow at twelve o'clock.

A vote was taken, but the Chair did not decide.

[Voices, "Ten o'clock," "ten o'clock."]

Mr. KALBFLEISCH, of New York, moved, as an amendment to the amendment, that eleven o'clock be inserted in the place of twelve.

Mr. BAILEY, of Massachusetts. I trust that the original motion will prevail, for the reason that there are a large number of people here who are desirous of getting through as soon as possible with the work of the Convention. Therefore, I hope that the hour of ten o'clock will prevail. [Applause.]

THE PRESIDENT. The amendment to the amendment is first in order.

The ayes and noes were taken, and the amendment to the amendment (fixing the hour at eleven o'clock) was lost.

THE PRESIDENT. Now the motion is upon the amendment fixing the hour at twelve o'clock.

The ayes and noes were taken and the amendment was lost.

The original motion was then put and carried.

Mr. FIRSCHING, of Pennsylvania. I have a memorial prepared by gentlemen in my Congressional district, which I wish to have referred to the Committee on Resolutions. I wish to have it referred without a reading.

The memorial was referred to that committee under the rule.

Mr. BABCOCK, of Connecticut. I beg leave to refer to the Committee on Resolutions the resolution which I hold in my hand. Referred to the Committee on Resolutions.

Mr. BABCOCK, of Connecticut. I have a brief statement to make to the Convention.

ADDRESS OF SOUTHERN DELEGATES, NATIVES OF NEW ENGLAND, TO THE PEOPLE OF NEW ENGLAND.

The members of the Louisiana, Mississippi, and Missouri delegations, who were born in New England, have prepared an address to the people of New England and to the people of the whole North, with the consent of this Convention. That address, beautiful in its expression, eloquent in its appeal, and full of patriotism, and of the earnest purpose that animates all our hearts, has been read to us of this Connecticut delegation, and by unanimous vote I have been requested to move that that address may be made a part of the proceedings of this Convention. I therefore move you, sir, that the address be referred to the Committee on Resolutions and Address, and be read to this Convention, and form a part of these proceedings. [Voices, "Good," "good."] It was referred to the committee.

ADJOURNMENT.

Mr. ORR, of South Carolina. I move that the Convention do now adjourn.

A vote was taken and the motion carried. The Convention then adjourned to meet again to-morrow morning at ten o'clock.

THIRD DAY.

The Convention met pursuant to adjournment. At ten A. M. the Convention was called to order.

THE PRESIDENT. The Convention will please come to order, and the Rev. M. J. S. Reimensynder, of Lewistown, Pennsylvania, will open the proceedings with prayer.

THE PRAYER.

Lord God, Jehovah, King of Kings! We adore Thee as the first, the greatest, and the best of beings. Thou art the Author of this creation, both physical and spiritual. Thou art the Ruler of all the earth; the Sovereign of all things that are in Heaven above and on the earth beneath, visible and invisible, whether they be thrones or dominions, and principalities or powers; Thou art from everlasting to everlasting. Of old didst Thou lay the foundations of this earth, and give to the sea her depth, and stretch over our heads the glorious firmament rejoicing in its stars. Thou fillest the heavens with Thy presence, and immensity is Thy realm, and the eternal years the servants of Thy sceptre. How, then, can we, creatures of the dust and of a day, aspire to cast up our eyes, after our rebellion, unto Thee, save through the promises of Thy Son Jesus Christ, through that love and forbearance which knew no limits? For to save the chiefest of sinners Thou didst give the precious blood of Thine only beloved Son. We come trusting in and pleading this blood, asking that Thou will freely receive us, and not cast us, Thy children, off forever. We thank Thee that Thou didst make our pathway easier than before, and that Thou didst change the convenant of works to that of grace; so that we have gained, through Christ, more than lost through Adam. And yet, O Father, in the weakness of human wisdom, and the folly of human guilt, we have been in a great and fearful conflict against each other. Brother has striven against brother for the mastery, till the very heavens were shaken with the roar of our arms; fields are laid waste, and the battle's din raged for six years—six years of hardships and suffering in the tented field, upon the weary march, upon the field of battle. But we thank Thee that they come up now from the North and from the

South, from the East and from the West, to meet beneath the ægis of the American eagle; that they meet each other again with the loving, true hands of friends and of brethren. We adore and thank Thee for this great spectacle, and we confidently invoke Thy presence and Thy sanction to rest upon the great work now imposed upon this, the most august of American assemblies. Crown its deliberations with holy wisdom; sanctify them with Thy love; harmonize them for peace; make them fit to right the woes of this great people. Let Thy blessings especially rest upon the President of the United States, in his efforts to vindicate the Constitution and render this great American nation imperishable throughout future generations. And do Thou grant, O Lord, that its future may ever, as now, be decided on the fields of talent, and not on the contested grounds of the sword. And now we commit humbly, and yet trustingly, our great country, our great people, and our common destiny into the keeping of the adorable Trinity of Heaven—Father, Son, and Holy Spirit—world without end. Amen.

THE PRESIDENT. Gentlemen will now resume their seats and the Convention be in order. Before proceeding to any further business, the Chair begs leave to announce, as the first response to our action, the result of the Colarado election. [Great cheers.] Returns read:

COLORADO, August 15.—Returns from all parts of the Territory render certain the election of A. C. Hunt, Administration candidate, for Delegate to Congress, over Chillcot, the Radical candidate.

[Enthusiastic applause.]

MR. SMITH, of New Jersey. I beg to offer the following resolution:

THE PRESIDENT. The Secretary will read the resolution offered by the gentleman from New Jersey.

The Secretary then read the following:

NATIONAL UNION EXECUTIVE COMMITTEE.

Resolved, That a Union National Executive Committee be appointed, to be composed of two delegates from each State and Territory and the District of Columbia.

The resolution was unanimously adopted:

Hon. REVERDY JOHNSON. I wish to offer this resolution to the Convention.

THE PRESIDENT. The resolution will be read.

The Secretary read the following:

COMMITTEE TO PRESENT THE PROCEEDINGS TO THE PRESIDENT.

Resolved, That a committee of two from each State and one from each Territory of the United States; and one from the District of Columbia, be appointed by the Chair to wait upon the President of the United States and present him with an authentic copy of the proceedings of this Convention.

[Cheers.]

The resolution was unanimously adopted.

CHARLES KNAP, Esq. I offer the following resolution.

[Cheers.]

THE PRESIDENT. The Secretary will read the resolution. The Convention will come to order.

The Secretary read the following:

COMMITTEE ON FINANCE.

Resolved, That a committee on finance be appointed, to consist of two delegates from each State and Territory and from the District of Columbia.

The resolution was unanimously adopted.

GENERAL PATTERSON, of Pennsylvania. I have been informed that my name has been added to the list of delegates, and as I understand there was a contestant for the seat, I beg to offer the following resolution, and ask that it be read:

THE PRESIDENT. It must be referred to the Committee on Resolutions.

Hon. EDGAR COWAN. I beg to offer the following resolution:

THE PRESIDENT. The resolution will be read.

The Secretary read the following:

THANKS TO THE MAYOR OF PHILADELPHIA.

Resolved, That the thanks of this Convention are due, and are hereby tendered, Morton McMichael, Mayor of the city of Philadelphia, for his admirable police arrangements for the preservation of peace and good order during the session of this Convention.

The resolution was unanimously adopted.

REPORT OF COMMITTEE ON RESOLUTIONS AND ADDRESS.

Hon. Edgar Cowan. On behalf of the committee appointed to prepare resolutions and an address, after a very careful and elaborate consideration of the subject, lasting all the day and a good part of the night, I beg leave to report the following declaration of principles, adopted unanimously by the committee, which will be read to the Convention; and also the address to the people of the country, which will be read by the Hon. Mr. Raymond, of New York.

The President. The gentleman from Pennsylvania offers the following declaration of principles and accompanying resolutions, which will now be read:

The Secretary then read as follows:

DECLARATION OF PRINCIPLES.

The National Union Convention, now assembled in the city of Philadelphia, composed of delegates from every State and Territory in the Union, admonished by the solemn lessons which, for the last five years, it has pleased the Supreme Ruler of the Universe to give to the American people; profoundly grateful for the return of peace; desirous, as are a large majority of their countrymen, in all sincerity, to forget and forgive the past; revering the Constitution as it comes to us from our ancestors; regarding the Union in its restoration as more sacred than ever; looking with deep anxiety into the future, as of instant and continuing trials, hereby issues and proclaims the following declaration of principles and purposes, on which they have, with perfect unanimity, agreed:

1st. We hail with gratitude to Almighty God the end of the war and the return of peace to our afflicted and beloved land.

2d. The war just closed has maintained the authority of the Constitution, with all the powers which it confers, and all the restrictions which it imposes upon the General Government, unabridged and unaltered, and it has preserved the Union, with the equal rights, dignity, and authority of the States perfect and unimpaired.

3d. Representation in the Congress of the United States and in the Electoral College is a right recognized by the Constitution as abiding in every State, and as a duty imposed upon the people, fundamental in its nature, and essential to the existence of our republican institutions, and neither Congress nor the General Government has any authority or power to deny this right to any State or to withhold its enjoyment under the Constitution from the people thereof.

4th. We call upon the people of the United States to elect to Congress as members thereof none but men who admit this fundamental right of representation, and who will receive to seats therein loyal representatives from every State in allegiance to the United States, subject to the constitutional right of each House to judge of the elections, returns, and qualifications of its own members.

5th. The Constitution of the United States, and the laws made in pursuance thereof, are the supreme law of the land, anything in the constitution or laws of any State to the contrary notwithstanding. All the powers not conferred by the Constitution upon the General Government, nor prohibited by it to the States, are reserved to the States, or to the people thereof; and among the rights thus reserved to the States is the right to prescribe qualifications for the elective franchise therein, with which right Congress cannot interfere. No State or combination of States has the right to withdraw from the Union, or to exclude, through their action in Congress or otherwise, any other State or States from the Union. The Union of these States is perpetual.

6th. Such amendments to the Constitution of the United States may be made by the people thereof as they may deem expedient, but only in the mode pointed out by its provisions; and in proposing such amendments, whether by Congress or by a Convention, and in ratifying the same, all the States of the Union have an equal and an indefeasible right to a voice and a vote thereon.

7th. Slavery is abolished and forever prohibited, and there is neither desire nor purpose on the part of the Southern States that it should ever be re-established upon the soil, or within the jurisdiction of the United States; and the enfranchised slaves in all the States of the Union should receive, in common with all their inhabitants, equal protection in every right of person and property.

8th. While we regard as utterly invalid, and never to be assumed or made of binding force, any obligations incurred or undertaken in making war against the United States, we hold the debt of the Nation to be sacred and inviolable; and we proclaim our purpose in discharging this, as in performing all other national obligations, to maintain unimpaired and unimpeached the honor and the faith of the Republic.

9th. It is the duty of the National Government to recognize the services of the Federal soldiers and sailors in the contest just closed, by meeting promptly and fully all their just and rightful claims for the services they have rendered the Nation, and by extending to those of them who have survived, and to the widows and orphans of those who have fallen, the most generous and considerate care.

10th. In Andrew Johnson, President of the United States, who, in his great office, has proved steadfast in his devotion to the Constitution, the laws, and interests of his country, unmoved by persecution and undeserved reproach, having faith unassailable in the people and in the principles of free government, we recognize a Chief Magistrate worthy of the Nation and equal to the great crisis upon which his lot is cast; and we tender to him, in the discharge of his high and responsible duties, our profound respect and assurance of our cordial and sincere support.

The resolutions were unanimously adopted.

A DELEGATE from Pennsylvania. I propose three cheers for the Hon. Edgar Cowan.

ENTHUSIASTIC CHEERS FOR HON. EDGAR COWAN.

Three hearty cheers were here given, the whole audience rising to their feet and heartily responding.

GENERAL W. PATTEN, of Pennsylvania. I propose three more for Mr. Cowan.

This was responded to in like manner.

MR. COWAN'S RESPONSE.

Mr. COWAN, of Pennsylvania.—Mr. President and Gentlemen of the Convention: I claim to be the host of the Convention, and one of my distinguished guests will now address you, and address you by virtue of authority unanimously derived from the Committee on Resolutions and Address—the Hon. Mr. Raymond. [Applause.]

THE PRESIDENT. The Hon. Mr. Raymond, from the State of New York, will now read the address, which has received the unanimous approval of the Committee on Resolutions and Address. [Applause.]

Mr. RAYMOND then stepped forward, amid deafening cheers, which, having somewhat subsided, he read as follows:

THE PRESIDENT. The Hon. H. J. Raymond will now read the address.

The Hon. H. J. RAYMOND then read as follows:

THE ADDRESS.

To the People of the United States:

Having met in Convention at the city of Philadelphia, in the State of Pennsylvania, this 16th day of August, 1866, as the representatives of the people in all sections and all the States and Territories of the Union, to consult upon the condition and the wants of our common country, we address to you this declaration of our principles and of the political purposes we seek to promote.

Since the meeting of the last National Convention, in the year 1860, events have occurred which have changed the character of our internal policy, and given the United States a new place among the nations of the earth. Our Government has passed through the vicissitudes and the perils of civil war—a war which, though mainly sectional in its character, has nevertheless decided political differences that from the very beginning of the Government had threatened the unity of our national existence, and has left its impress, deep and ineffaceable, upon all the interests, the sentiments, and the destiny of the Republic. While it has inflicted upon the whole country severe losses in life and in property, and has imposed burdens which must weigh on its resources for generations to come, it has developed a degree of noble courage in the presence of national dangers, a capacity for military organization and achievment, and devotion on the part of the people to the form of government which they have ordained, and to the principles of liberty which that Government was designed to promote, which must confirm the confidence of the Nation in the perpetuity of its republican institutions, and command the respect of the civilized world. Like all great contests which rouse the passions and test the endurance of nations, this war has given new scope to the ambition of political parties, and fresh impulse to plans of innovation and reform. Amidst the chorus of conflicting sentiments, inseparable from such an era, while the public heart is keenly alive to all the passions that can sway the public judgment and affect the public action, while the wounds of war are still fresh and bleeding on either side, and fears for the future take unjust proportions from the memories and resentments of the past, it is a difficult, but an imperative duty which, in your behalf, we who are here asembled have undertaken to perform. For the first time after six long years of alienation and of conflict, we have come together from every State and every section of our land, as citizens of a common country, under that flag, the symbol again of a common glory, to consult together how best to secure and perpetuate that Union which is again the object of our common love, and thus secure the blessings of liberty to ourselves and our posterity.

In the first place, we invoke you to remember, always and everywhere, that the war is ended, and the nation is again at peace. The shock of contending arms no longer assails the shuddering heart of the Republic. The insurrection against the supreme authority of the nation has been suppressed, and that authority has been again acknowledged by word and act in every State and by every citizen within its jurisdiction. We are no longer required or permitted to regard or treat each other as enemies. Not only have the acts of war been discontinued, and the weapons of war laid aside, but the state of war no longer exists, and the sentiments, the passions, the relations of war have no longer lawful or rightful place anywhere throughout our broad dominion. We are again people of the United States, fellow-citizens of one country, bound by the duties and obligations of a common nation, and having neither rights nor interests apart from a common destiny. The duties that devolve upon us now are again the duties of peace, and no longer the duties of war. We have assembled here to take counsel concerning the interests of peace, to decide how we may most wisely and effectually heal the wounds the war has made, and perfect and perpetuate the benefits it has secured, and the blessings which, under a wise and benign Providence, sprung up in its fiery track. This is the work not of passion, but of calm and sober judgment; not of resentment for past offences, prolonged beyond the limits which justice and reason prescribe, but of a liberal statesmanship which tolerates what it cannot prevent, and builds its plans and its hopes for the future rather upon a community of interest and ambition than upon distrust and the weapons of force.

In the next place, we call upon you to recognize, in their full significance, and to accept, with all their legitimate consequences, the political results of the war just closed. In two most important particulars the victory achieved by the National Government has been final and decisive—first: it has established, beyond all further controversy, and by the highest of all human sanction, the absolute supremacy of the National Government, as defined and directed by the Constitution of the United States, and the permanent integrity and indissolubility of the Federal Union is a necessary consequence; and secondly, it has put an end, finally and forever, to the existence of slavery upon the soil or within the jurisdiction of the United States. Both these points became directly involved in the contest, and controversy upon both has ended absolutely and finally by the result.

In the third place, we deem it of the utmost importance that the real character of the war, and the victory by which it was closed, should be accurately understood. The war was carried on by the Government of the United States in maintenance of its own authority, and in defence of its own existence, both of which were menaced by the insurrection which it sought to suppress. The suppression of that insurrection accomplished that result. The Government of the United States maintained by force of arms the supreme authority over all the territory and over all the States and people within its jurisdiction which the Constitution confers upon it; but it acquired thereby no new power, no enlarged jurisdiction, no rights, either of territorial possession or of civil authority, which it did not possess before the rebellion broke out. All the rightful power it can ever possess is that which is conferred upon it in express terms, or by fair and necessary implication, by the Constitution of the United States. It was that power and that authority which the rebellion sought to overthrow, and the victory of the Federal arms was simply the defeat of that attempt.

The Government of the United States acted throughout the war on the defensive. It sought only to hold possession of what was already its own. Neither the war, nor the victory by which it was ended, changed in any way the Constitution of the United States. The war was carried on by virtue of its provisions and under the limitations which they prescribed, and the result of the war did not either enlarge, abridge, or in any way change or affect the powers it confers upon the Federal Government, or release that Government from the restrictions which it has imposed.

The Constitution of the United States is to-day precisely as it was before the war—the supreme law of the land, anything in the constitution or laws of any State to the contrary notwithstanding. And to-day also, precisely as before the war, all the powers not conferred by the Constitution upon the General Government, nor prohibited by it to the States, are reserved to the several States or to the people thereof.

This position is vindicated not only by the essential nature of our Government and the language and spirit of the Constitution, but by all the acts and the language of our Government, in all its departments and at all times, from the outbreak of the rebellion to its final overthrow. In the messages and proclamations of the Executive it was explicitly declared that the sole object and purpose of the war was to maintain the authority of the Constitution and to preserve the integrity of the Union, and Congress more than once reiterated this solemn declaration, and added the assurance, that whenever this object should be attained the war should cease, and all the States should retain their equal rights and dignity unimpaired. It is only since the war has closed that other rights have been asserted on behalf of one department of the General Government. It has been proclaimed by Congress that, in addition to the powers conferred upon it by the Constitution, the Federal Government may now claim over the States and the territory, and the people involved in the insurrection, the rights of war—right of conquest and of confiscation, the right to abrogate all existing governments, institutions, and laws, and to subject the territory conquered and its inhabitants to such terms and regulations as the legislative department of the Government may see fit to impose, under the broad and sweeping claim that the clause of the Constitution which provides that no State shall, without its consent, be deprived of its equal suffrage in the Senate of the United States, has been annulled; and States have been refused, and are still refused, representation altogether in both branches of the Federal Congress; and the Congress in which only a part of the States and of the people of the Union are represented has asserted the right to exclude others from representation and from all share in making their own laws and choosing their own rulers, unless they shall comply with such conditions and perform such acts as this Congress, thus composed, may itself prescribe. That right has not only been asserted, but it has been exercised, and is practically enforced at the present time. Nor does it find any support in the cry that the States thus excluded are in rebellion against the Government, and are therefore precluded from sharing its authority. They are not thus in rebellion. They are one and all in an attitude of loyalty towards the Government, and of sworn allegiance to the Constitution of the United States. In none of them is there the slightest indication of resistance to this authority, or the slightest protest against its just and binding obligations. This condition of renewed loyalty has been officially recognized by solemn proclamation of the Executive Department. The laws of the United States have been extended by Congress over all these States, and the people thereof. Federal courts have been reopened, and Federal taxes imposed and levied, and in every respect, except that they are denied representation in Congress and the Electoral College, the States once in rebellion are recognized as holding the same obligations and subject to the same duties as the other States of our common Union.

It seems to us, in the exercise of the calmest and most candid judgment we can bring to the subject, such a claim so enforced involves as fatal an overthrow of the authority of the Constitution, and as complete a destruction of the Government and Union, as that which was sought to be effected by the States and people in armed insurrection against them. It cannot escape observation, that the power thus asserted to exclude certain States from representation is made to rest wholly in the will and discretion of the Congress that asserts it. It is not made to depend upon specified conditions or circumstances, not to be subject to any rules or regulations whatever. The right asserted and exercised is absolute, without qualification or restriction, not confined to States in rebellion, nor to States that have rebelled. It is the right of any Congress, in formal possession of legislative authority, to exclude any State or States, and any portion of the people thereof, at any time from representation in Congress, and in the Electoral College, at its own discretion, and until they shall perform such acts and comply with such conditions as it may dictate. Obviously, the reasons for such exclusion being wholly within the discretion of Congress, may change as the Congress itself shall change.

One Congress may exclude a State from all share in the Government for one reason and that reason removed, the next Congress may exclude it for another. One State may be excluded on one ground to-day, and another may be excluded on the opposite ground to-morrow. Northern ascendency may exclude Southern States from Congress—the ascendency of Western or Southern interests, or of both combined, may exclude the Northern or the Eastern States from the next.

Improbable as such usurpations may seem, the establishment of the principles now asserted and acted upon by Congress will render them by no means impossible. The character, indeed, the very existence of Congress and the Union, is thus made dependent solely and entirely upon the party and sectional exigencies or forbearance of the hour. We need not stop to show that such action not only finds no warrant in the Constitution, but is at war with every principle of our Government and with the very existence of free institutions. It is, indeed, the identical practice which has rendered fruitless all attempts hitherto to establish and maintain free governments in Mexico and the States of South America. Party necessities assert themselves as superior to fundamental law, which is set aside in reckless obedience to their behests. Stability, whether in the exercise of power in the administration of government or in the enjoyment of rights, becomes impossible, and the conflicts of party, which under constitutional government are the conditions and means of political progress, are merged in the conflicts of arms, to which they directly and inevitably tend.

It was against this peril, so conspicuous, and so fatal to all free governments, that our Constitution was intended especially to provide. Not only the stability, but the very existence of the Government is made by its provisions to depend upon the right and the fact of representation. The Congress, upon which is conferred all the legislative power of National Government, consists of two branches—the Senate and House of Representatives—whose joint concurrence or assent is essential to the validity of any law. Of these the House of Representatives, says the Constitution, (Article 1st, section 2d,) shall be composed of members chosen every second year by the people of the several States. Not only is the right of representation thus recognized as possessed by all the States and by every State, without restriction, qualification, or condition of any kind, but the duty of choosing Representatives is imposed upon the people of each and every State alike, without distinction or the authority to make distinction among them for any reason or upon any grounds whatever.' And in the Senate, so careful is the Constitution to secure to every State this right of representation, it is expressly provided that no State shall, without its consent, be deprived of its equal suffrage in that body, even by amendment to the Constitution itself. When, therefore, any State is excluded from such representation, not only is the right of the State denied, but the constitutional integrity of the Senate is impaired, and the validity of the Government itself is brought in question. But Congress at the present moment thus excludes from representation in both branches of Congress ten States of the Union, denying them all share in the enactment of laws by which they are to be governed, and all participation in the election of the rulers by which those laws are to be enforced. In other words, a Congress in which only twenty-six States are represented asserts the right to govern, absolutely and in its own discretion, all the thirty-six States which compose the Union; to make their laws and choose their rulers, and to exclude the other ten from all share in their own government, until it sees fit to admit them thereto. What is there to distinguish the power thus asserted and exercised from the most absolute and intolerate tyranny? Nor do these extravagant and unjust claims on the part of Congress to powers and authority never conferred upon the Government by the Constitution, find any warrant in the arguments or excuses urged on their behalf. It is alleged—

First. That these States, by the act of rebellion and by voluntarily withdrawing their members from Congress, forfeited their right of representation, and that they can only receive it again at the hands of the supreme legislative authority of the Government, on its own terms and at its own discretion. If representation in Congress, and participation in the Government, were simply privileges conferred and held by favor, this statement might have the merit of plausibility. But representation is, under the Constitution, not only expressly recognized as a right, but it is imposed as a duty, and it is essential in both aspects to the existence of the Government and to the maintenance of its authority. In free Governments fundamental and essential rights cannot be forfeited, except against individuals by due process of law; nor can constitutional duties and obligations be discarded or laid aside. The enjoyment of rights may be for a time suspended by the failure to claim them, and duties may be evaded by the refusal to perform them. The withdrawal of their members from Congress by the States which resisted the General Government was among their acts of insurrection—was one of the means and agencies by which they sought to impair the authority and defeat the action of the Government; and that act was annulled and rendered void when the insurrection itself was suppressed. Neither the right of representation nor the duty to be represented was in the least impaired by the fact of insurrection; but it may have been that, by reason of the insurrection, the conditions on which the enjoyment of that right and the permanence of that duty for the time depended could not be fulfilled. This was, in fact, the case. An insurgent power, in the exercise of usurped and unlawful authority in the territory under its control, had prohibited that allegiance to the Constitution and laws of the United States which is made by that fundamental law the essential condition of representation in Government. No man within the insurgent States was allowed to take the oath to support the Constitution of the United States, and, as a necessary consequence, no man could lawfully represent those States in the councils of the Union. But this was only an obstacle to the enjoyment of the right and to the discharge of a duty; it did not annul the one nor abrogate the other, and it ceased to exist when the usurpation by which it was created had been overthrown, and the States had again resumed their allegiance to the Constitution and laws of the United States.

Second. But it is asserted in support of the authority claimed by the Congress now in possession of power, that it flows directly from the laws of war; that it is among the rights which victorious war always confers upon the conquerors, and which the conqueror may exercise or waive, in his own discretion. To this we reply, that the laws in question relate solely, so far as the rights they confer are concerned, to wars waged between alien and independent nations, and can have no place or force in this regard in a war waged by a government to suppress an insurrection of its own people, upon its own soil, against its authority. If we had carried on successful war against any foreign nation, we might thereby have acquired possession and jurisdiction of their soil, with the right to enforce our laws upon their people, and to impose upon them such laws and such obligations as we might choose. But we had, before the war, complete jurisdiction over the soil of the Southern States, limited only by our own Constitution. Our laws were the only national laws in force upon it. The Government of the United States was the only Government through which those States and their people had relations with foreign nations, and its flag was the only flag by which they were recognized or known anywhere on the face of the earth. In all these respects, and in all other respects involving national interests and rights, our possession was perfect and complete. It did not need to be acquired, but only to be maintained; and victorious war against the rebellion could do nothing more than maintain it. It could only vindicate and reëstablish the disputed supremacy of the Constitution. It could neither enlarge nor diminish the authority which that Constitution confers upon the Government by which it was achieved. Such an enlargement or abridgment of constitutional power can be effected only by amendment of the Constitution itself, and such amendment can be made only in the modes which the Constitution itself prescribes.

The claim that the suppression of an insurrection against the Government gives additional authority and power to that Government, especially that it enlarges the jurisdiction of Congress and gives that body the right to exclude States from representation in the National Councils, without which the nation itself can have no authority and no existence, seems to us at variance alike with the principles of the Constitution and with the public safety.

Third. But it is alleged that in certain particulars the Constitution of the United States fails to secure the absolute justice and impartial equality which the principles of our Government require; that it was in these respects the result of compromises and concessions to which, however necessary when the Constitution was formed, we are no longer compelled to submit; and that now, having the power through successful war, and just warrant for its exercise in the hostile conduct of the insurgent section, the actual Government of the United States may impose its own conditions and make the Constitution conform in all its provisions to its own ideas of equality and the rights of war. Congress, at its last session, proposed amendments to the Constitution, enlarging, in some very important particulars, the authority of the General Government over that of the several States, and reducing, by indirect disfranchisement, the representative power of the States in which slavery formerly existed; and it is claimed that these amendments may be made valid as parts of the original Constitution without the concurrence of the States to be most seriously affected by them, or may be imposed upon those States by three-fourths of the remaining States, as conditions of their readmission to representation in Congress and in the Electoral College.

It is the unquestionable right of the people of the United States to make such changes in the Constitution as they upon due deliberation may deem expedient. But we insist that they shall be made in the mode which the Constitution itself points out, in conformity with the letter and spirit of that instrument, and with the principles of self-government and of equal rights which lie at the basis of our republican institutions. We deny the right of Congress to make these changes in the fundamental law without the concurrence of three-fourths of all the States, including especially those to be most seriously affected by them, or to impose them upon States or people as conditions of representation or of admission to any of the rights, duties, or obligations which belong, under the Constitution, to all the States alike; and with still greater emphasis do we deny the right of any portion of the States, excluding the rest of the States from any share in their councils, to propose or sanction changes in the Constitution which are to affect permanently their political relations, and control or coerce the legitimate action of the several members of the common Union. Such an exercise of power is simply a usurpation, just as unwarrantable when exercised by Northern States as it would be if exercised by Southern, and not to be fortified or palliated by anything in the past history either of those by whom it is attempted or of those upon whose rights and liberties it is to take effect. It finds no warrant in the Constitution. It is at war with the fundamental principles of our form of government. If tolerated in one instance it becomes the precedent for future invasions of liberty and constitutional right, dependent solely upon the will of the party in possession of power, and thus leads by direct and necessary sequence to the most fatal and intolerable of all tyrannies, the tyranny of shifting and irresponsible political factions. It is against this, the most formidable of all the dangers which menace the stability of free government, that the Constitution of the United States was intended most carefully to provide. We demand a strict and steadfast adherence to its provisions. In this, and in this alone, can we find a basis of permanent union and peace.

Fourth. But it is alleged, in justification of the usurpation which we condemn, that the condition of the Southern States and people is not such as renders safe their re-admission to a share in the government of the country; that they are still disloyal in sentiment and purpose, and that neither the honor, the credit, nor the interests of the Nation would be safe if they were re-admitted to share in its councils. We might reply to this—

First. That we have no right for such reasons to deny to any portion of the States or people rights expressly conferred upon them by the Constitution of the United States.

Second. That so long as their acts are those of loyalty; so long as they conform in all their public conduct to the requirements of the Constitution and laws, we have no right to exact from them conformity to their sentiments and opinions to our own.

Third. That we have no right to distrust the purpose or the ability of the people of the Union to protect and defend, under all contingencies, and by whatever means may be required, its honor and its welfare. These would, in our judgment, be full and conclusive answers to the plea thus advanced for the exclusion of these States from the Union. But we say, further, that this plea rests upon a complete misapprehension, or an unjust perversion of existing facts. We do not hesitate to affirm that there is no section of the country where the Constitution and laws of the United States find a more prompt and entire obedience than in those States and among those people who were lately in arms against them, or where there is less purpose or danger of any future attempt to overthrow their authority.

It would seem to be rational and inevitable that in States and sections so recently swept by the whirlwind of war, where all the ordinary modes and methods of organized industry have been broken up, and the bonds and influence that guarantee social order have been destroyed; where thousands and tens of thousands of turbulent spirits have been suddenly loosed from the discipline of war, and thrown without resources or restraint upon a disorganized and chaotic society, and when the keen sense of defeat is added to the overthrow of ambition and hope, scenes of violence should defy for a time the imperfect discipline of law and excite anew the fears and forebodings of the patriotic and well disposed. It is unquestionably true that local disturbances of this kind, accompanied by more or less of violence, do still occur. But they are confined entirely to the cities and larger towns of the Southern States, where different races and interests are brought most closely in contact, and where passions and resentment are always most easily fed and fanned into outbreak; and even that they are quite as much the fruit of untimely and hurtful political agitation, as of any hostility on the part of the people to the authority of the National Government. But the concurrent testimony of those best acquainted with the condition of society and the state of public sentiment in the South, including that of its representatives in this Convention, establishes the fact that the great mass of the Southern people accept, with as full and sincere submission as do the people of the other States, the re-established supremacy of the national authority, and are prepared, in the most loyal spirit, and with a zeal quickened alike by their interest and their pride, and co-operate with other States and sections in whatever may be necessary to defend the rights, maintain the honor, and promote the welfare of our common country.

History affords no instance where a people so powerful in numbers, in resources, and in public spirit, after a war so long in its duration, so destructive in its progress, and so adverse in its issue, have accepted defeat and its consequences with so much of good faith as has marked the conduct of the people lately in insurrection against the United States. Beyond all question this has been largely due to the wise generosity with which their enforced surrender was accepted by the President of the United States, and the generals in immediate command of our armies, and to the liberal measures which were afterwards taken to restore order, tranquillity, and law, to the States where all had for the time been overthrown. No step could have been better calculated to command the respect, win the confidence, revive the patriotism, and secure the permanent and affectionate allegiance of the people of the South to the Constitution and laws of the Union than those which have been so firmly taken and so steadfastly pursued by the President of the United States.

And if that confidence and loyalty has been since impaired, if the people South are to-day less candid in that allegiance than they were immediately upon the close of the war, we believe it is due to the changed tone of the Legislative Department of the General Government towards them; to the action by which Congress has endeavored to suppress and defeat the President's wise and beneficial policy of restoration; to their exclusion from all participation in our common Government; to the withdrawal from them of the rights conferred and guaranteed by the Constitution, and to the evident purpose of Congress, in the exercise of an usurped and unlawful authority, to reduce them from the ranks of free and equal members of a republic of States, with rights and dignities unimpaired, to the condition of conquered provinces and a conquered people, in all things subservient and subject to the will of their conquerors, free only to obey laws in making which they are not allowed to share. No people has ever yet existed whose loyalty and faith such treatment, long continued, would not alienate and impair. And the ten millions of Americans who live in the South would be unworthy citizens of a free country, degenerate sons of an heroic ancestry—unfit ever to become guardians of the rights and liberties bequeathed to us by the fathers and founders of this Republic—if they could accept, with uncomplaining submissiveness, the humiliations thus sought to be imposed upon them. Resentment of injustice is always and everywhere essential to freedom, and the spirit which prompts the States and people lately in insurrection—insurgents now no longer—to protest against the imposition of unjust and degrading conditions, makes them all the more worthy to share in the government of a free commonwealth, and gives still firmer assurance of the future power and freedom of the Republic; for whatever responsibility the Southern people may have incurred in resisting the authority of the National Government, and in taking up arms for its overthrow, they may be held to answer for as individuals before the judicial tribunals of the land, and for their conduct as societies and organized communities they have already paid the most fearful penalty that can fall on offending States, in the losses, the sufferings, and humiliations of unsuccessful war. But whatever may be the guilt or the punishment of the conscious authors of the insurrection, candor and common justice demand concession to the great mass of those who became involved in its risks, and acted upon what they deemed to be their duty, and in defence of what they had been taught to believe were their rights, or under a compulsion, physical and moral, which they were powerless to resist. Nor can it be amiss to remember that, terrible as have been the bereavements and the losses of this war, they have fallen exclusively upon neither section and upon neither party; that they have fallen, indeed, with far greater weight upon those with whom the war begun; that in the death of relatives and friends, the dispersion of families, the disruption of social systems and social ties, the overthrow of governments, of law and of order, the destruction of property and of forms and modes and means of industry, the loss of political, commercial, and moral influence in any shape and form—which great calamities we are sure the States and people which engaged in the war against the Government of the United States have suffered tenfold more than those who remained in allegiance to its Constitution and laws. These considerations may not, as they certainly do not, justify the action of the people of the insurgent States; but no humane, generous mind will refuse to them very considerable weight in determining the line of conduct which the Government of the United States should pursue towards them. They accept, if not with alacrity, certainly without sullen resentment, the defeat and overthrow they have sustained. They acknowledge and acquiesce in the results to themselves and the country which that defeat involves; they no longer claim for any State the right to secede from the Union; they no longer assert for any State an allegiance paramount to that which is due to the General Government. They have accepted the destruction of slavery—abolished it by their State constitutions—and concurred with the States and people of the whole Union in prohibiting its existence forever upon the soil or within the jurisdiction of the United States. They indicate and evince their purpose, just so fast as may be possible and safe, to adapt their domestic laws to the changed condition of their society, and to secure by the law and its tribunals equal and impartial justice to all classes of their inhabitants. They admit the invalidity of all acts of resistance to the national authority and of all debts incurred in attempting its overthrow. They avow their willingness to share the burdens and discharge all the duties and obligations which rest upon them in common with other States and other sections of the Union; and they renew, through their representatives in this Convention, by all their public conduct in every way, and by the more solemn acts by which States and societies can pledge their faith and allegiance, through all time to come, to the Constitution of the Uuited States, and to all laws which may be made in pursuance thereof.

Fellow-countrymen, we call upon you, in full reliance upon your intelligence and your patriotism, to accept with generous and ungrudging confidence the full surrender on the part of those lately in arms against your authority, and to share with them the honor and renown that await those who bring back peace and concord to jarring States. The war just closed, with its sorrows and disasters, has opened a new career of glory to the nation it has saved. It has swept away the hostilities of sentiment and of interest which were a standing menace to its peace. It has destroyed the institution of slavery, always a cause of sectional agitation and strife, and has opened for our country the way to unity of interest, of principle, and of action through all time to come. It has developed in both sections a military capacity and aptitute for achievements of war, both by sea and by land, before unknown even to ourselves, and destined to exercise hereafter, under united councils, an important influence upon the character and destiny of the continent and the world. And while it has thus revealed, disciplined, compacted our power, it has proven to us, beyond controversy or doubt, by the course pursued towards both contending sections by foreign powers, that we must be the guardans of our own independence, and that the principles of republican freedom we represent can find among the nations of the earth no friends or defenders but ourselves.

We call upon you, therefore, by every consideration of your own dignity and safety, and in the name of liberty throughout the world, to complete the work of restoration and peace which the President of the United States has so well begun, and by which the policy adopted and the principles asserted by the present Congress alone obstruct.

The time is close at hand when the members of a new Congress are to be elected. If that Congress shall perpetuate this policy, and by excluding loyal States and people from representation in its halls shall continue the usurpation by which the legislative powers of the Government are now exercised, common prudence compels us to anticipate augmented discontent, a sullen withdrawal from the duties and obligations of the Federal Government, internal dissension, and a general collision of sentiments and pretensions which may renew in a still more fearful shape the civil war from which we have just emerged We call upon you to interpose your power to prevent the recurrence of so transcendent a calamity. We call upon you in every Congresssional district of every State to secure the election of members who, whatever other difference may characterize their political action, will unite in recognizing the right of every State of the Union to representation in Congress, and who will admit to seats in either branch of every loyal Representative from every State in allegiance to the Government who may be found by each House, in the exercise of the power conferred upon it by the Constitution, to have been duly elected, returned, and qualified for a seat therein.

When this shall have been done, the Government will have been restored to its integrity, the Constitution of the United States will have been re-established in its full supremacy, and the American Union will have again become what it was designed to be by those who formed it—a sovereign nation, composed of separate States, like itself moving in a distinct and independent sphere, exercising powers defined and reserved by a common Constitution, and resting upon the assent, the confidence, and co-operation of all the States and all the people subject to its authority. Thus reorganized and restored to their constitutional relations, the States and the General Government can enter in a fraternal spirit, with a common purpose and a common interest, upon whatever reforms the security of personal rights, the enlargement of personal liberty, and the perfection of our republican institutions may demand.

APPOINTMENT OF COMMITTEES.

The Chair here announced the following names as constituting the National Union Executive Committee, the resident Executive Committee at Washington, the Committee to Wait on the President, and the Financial Committee :

COMMITTEE TO WAIT ON THE PRESIDENT.

Hon. REVERDY JOHNSON, Chairman ; Maine, W. G. Crosby, Calvin Record ; New Hampshire, J. Hosley, J. H. Smith ; Vermont, L. Robinson, General Isaac McDaniel ; Massachusetts, E. C. Bailey, Edward Avery ; Rhode Island, Amasa Sprague, Gideon Bradford ; Connecticut, Jas. E. English, G. H. Hollister ; New York, Vivus W. Smith, S. E. Church ; New Jersey, T. H. Herring, General Theodore Runyon ; Pennsylvania, J. R. Flanigan, George W. Cass ; Delaware, Saxe-Gotha Laws, C. H. B. Day ; Maryland, J. Morrison Harris, Isaac D. Jones ; Virginia, Hon. James Barbour, G. W. Bolling ; West Virginia, John J. Thompson, Daniel Lamb ; North Carolina, D. M. Barringer, G. Howard ; South Carolina, J. L. Manning, James Farrow ; Georgia, S. J. Smith, J. L. Wimberly ; Florida, J. P. Sanderson, J. C. McKibben ; Mississippi, Giles M. Hillyer, H. F. Simrall ; Louisiana, T. P. May, William H. C. King ; Texas, D. J. Burnett, B. H. Epperson ; Tennessee, A. A. Kyle, D. B. Thomas : Arkansas, John B. Luce, E. C. Boudinot ; Alabama, Lewis E. Parsons, John Gill Shorter; Kentucky, J. W. Stephenson, A. Harding ; Ohio, Henry B. Paine, General A. McD. McCook ; Indiana, General Sol. Meredith, David S. Gooding ; Illinois, General George C. Bates, Hon. W. R. Morrison ; Michigan, General C. O.

Loomis, General G. A. Custer; Wisconsin, A. W. Curtis, Robert Flint; Iowa, Colonel Cyrus H. Mackey, B. B. Richards; Kansas, General H. S. Sleeper, Orlin Thurston; California, J. A. McDougall, Colonel Jacob P. Leese; Nevada, Gideon J. Tucker, John Carmichael; Oregon, W. H. Farrar, E. M. Barnum; District of Columbia, Thomas B. Florence, B. T. Swart; Idaho, Hon. H. H. DePuy, S. Cummins; Nebraska, George L. Miller, L. Lowrie; Washington, George D. Cole, C. P. Egan; Minnesota, H. M. Rice, D. S. Norton; Missouri, E. A. Lewis, John M. Richardson; Dakotah, D. T. Bramble, L. D. Parmer.

NATIONAL UNION EXECUTIVE COMMITTEE.

Joseph T. Crowell, Chairman; Maine, James Mann, A. P. Gould; New Hampshire, Edmund Burke, E. S. Cutter; Vermont, B. D. Smalley, Colonel H. N. Worthan; Massachusetts, Josiah Dunham, R. S. Spofford; Rhode Island, Alfred Anthony, James H. Parsons; Connecticut, James T. Babcock, D. C. Scranton; New York, Robert H. Pruyn, Samuel J, Tilden; Pennsylvania, S. M. Zulick, J. S. Black; Delaware, J. P. Comegys, E. L. Martin; Maryland, T. Swann, T. D. Pratt; Virginia, J. F. Johnson, E. C. Robinson; West Virginia, Daniel Lamb, John J. Jackson; North Carolina, T. S. Ashe, Joseph H. Wilson; South Carolina, J. L. Orr, B. F. Perry; Georgia, J. H. Christie, T. Hardeman jr.; Florida, Hon. William Marvin, Hon. Wilkinson Call; Alabama, M. H. Cruikshank, C. C. Huckabee; Mississippi, William L. Sharkey, G. L. Potter; Louisiana, Randall Hunt, Alfred Hennen; Arkansas, Lorenzo Gibson, E. H. English; Texas, B. H. Epperson, John Hancock; Tennessee, Hon. David T. Patterson, W. D. Campbell; Kentucky, R. H. Stanton, Hamilton Pope; Ohio, Lewis D. Campbell, George B. Smythe; Indiana, Hon. David S. Gooding, T. Dowling; Illinois, General J. A. McClernand, J. O. Norton; Michigan, Alfred Russell, Byron G. Stout; Missouri, Barton Able, James S. Rollins; Minnesota, H. M. Rice, D. S. Norton; Wisconsin, S. A. Pease, J. A. Noonan; Iowa, George H. Parker, William A. Chase; Kansas, James L. McDowell, W. A. Tipton; New Jersey, Joseph T. Crowell, Theo. F. Randolph; Nevada, John Carmichael, G. B. Hall; District of Columbia, J. D. Hoover, J. B. Blake; Nebraska, H. H. Heath, J. S. Morton, Washington Territory, R. Willard, Elwood Evans; California, Samuel Purdy, Joseph P. Hoge; Oregon, J. W. Nesmith, B. F. Bonham; Dakota, W. K. Armstrong, N. W. Miner; Idaho, William H. Wallace, Henry Cummins.

RESIDENT EXECUTIVE COMMITTEE AT WASHINGTON.

Charles Knap, Chairman; Hon. Montgomery Blair, Hon. Charles Mason, Ward H. Lamon, John F. Coyle, A. E. Perry, Samuel Fowler, Colonel James R. O'Beirne, Cornelius Wendell.

COMMITTEE ON FINANCE.

Charles Knap, Chairman; Maine, A. W. Johnson, John Burleigh; New Hampshire, Daniel Marcy, W. N. Blair, Vermont, R. W. Chase, C. L. Davenport; Massachusetts, F. O. Prince, George M. Bentley; Rhode Island, Amasa Sprague, James Waterhouse; Connecticut, J. H. Ashmead, Freeman M. Brown; New York, Abraham Wakeman, Richard Schell; New Jersey, J. L. McKnght, Francis S. Lathrop; Pennsylvania, R. L. Martin, Henry M. Phillips; Delaware, Charles Wright, T. F. Crawford; Maryland, R. Fowler, W. P. Maulsby; Virginia, Edmund W. Hubbard, George Blow, Jr.; West Virginia, Charles T. Beale, Thomas Sweeney; North Carolina, A. H. Arrington, A. McLean; South Carolina, F. J. Moses, W. Pinkney Schingler; Georgia, Lewis Tumlin, William M. Lowry; Florida, George Scott, W. C. Maloney; Alabama, Lewis Owen, J. S. Kennedy; Mississippi, E. Pegues, J. A. Bingford; Louisiana, A. M. Holbrook; Arkansas, M. L. Bell, John R. Fellowes; Texas, M. B. Ochiltree, J. Hancock; Tennessee, W. B. Ferguson, J. Williams; Kentucky, M. J. Durham, W. W. Baldwin; Ohio, T. E. Cunningham, J. H. James; Indiana, Levi Sparks, Moses Drake; Illinois, William B. Ogden, Isaac Underhill; Michigan, G. C. Monroe, William B. McCreery; Missouri, Thomas L. Price, Charles M. Elliard; Minnesota, C. F. Buck, Charles F. Gilman; Wisconsin, J. B. Doe, C. L. Sholes; Iowa, W. D. McHenry, S. O. Butler; Kansas, T. P. Fitzwilliam, G. A. Colton; California, John H. Baird, Henry F. Williams; Nevada, Frank Hereford, L. H. Newton; District of Columbia, Charles Knap, Esau Pickrell; Dakota, J. B. S. Todd, F. C. Dewitt; Idaho, C. F. Powell, T. W. Betts; Nebraska, James R. Porter, P. B. Becker; Washington, Edward Lander, Elwood Evans; Oregon, J. C. Ainsworth, O. Hummason.

The Secretary having read the above list of committees—

Hon. John Hogan, of Missouri, said: Mr. President, this Convention, so glorious a success, has now accomplished the purpose for which it met, and I move, you, sir, in view of its harmonious action, that the Convention now adjourn. [Applause.]

THE PRESIDENT. Before putting that motion, the Chair desires to announce two or three things connected with what has transpired.

[At that point a slight confusion ensued, many members seeking to obtain a hearing.]

THE PRESIDENT. Let the Convention be in order.

THANKS TO THE OFFICERS OF THE CONVENTION.

Mr. SCHELL, of New York. I move that the thanks of this Convention be now tendered the President and the officers of this Convention, for the able and impartial manner in which they have discharged their duties. This motion was put by the Secretary and carried unanimously. [Applause.]

THANKS TO THE REPRESENTATIVES OF THE PRESS.

Mr. HOLMES, of New York. I think it eminently due to the representatives of the press who are present that the thanks of this Convention should be given them. A remarkable feature with their reportorial duties has been that each of them, of whatever complexion, whether for or against us, has manfully, correctly, and honestly performed his duty. [Applause.]

The consent of the Convention was obtained to the consideration of this motion, and it was unanimously carried.

PRESENT FROM THE PHILADELPHIA JOHNSON CLUB.

THE PRESIDENT. The Chair has received from the president, Geo. Martin, and C. W. Alexander, secretary, in behalf of the National Union Johnson Club of the city of Philadelphia, a gavel made of the wood of the frigate Constitution. [Applause.]

HONORARY MEMBERS FROM THE GERMAN JOHNSON CLUB OF NEW YORK.

The Chair is also requested to announce, that it may be entered in the proceedings, that the chairman of the German Johnson Central Club of the city of New York has presented several names as honorary members of the Convention, which will also take place in the proceedings and be published.

MEETING OF SOLDIER AND SAILOR DELEGATES.

I am requested to announce, in behalf of certain gentlemen, that there will be a number of the soldiers and sailors in attendance upon this Convention, in this place, at eight o'clock this evening. [Applause.]

THANKS TO THE CITIZENS OF PHILADELPHIA.

Hon. O. H. BROWNING, of Illinois. Mr. President, I move you, sir, that the thanks of this Convention be extended to the citizens of Philadelphia for their hospitality and kindness to its members during its deliberations.

A voice, "Good, I second the motion." [Applause.]

A vote was taken upon this motion, and it was unanimously carried.

The SECRETARY. I am requested to announce by the chairman of the committee appointed to wait upon the President, that the committee will meet at parlor C at the Continental Hotel at 3 o'clock this afternoon, and that the National Executive Committee will meet at room No. 17 at the Continental Hotel shortly after the adjournment.

Hon. REVERDY JOHNSON, of Maryland, offered the following resolution, which was read by the Secretary and unanimously passed by the Convention.

PUBLICATION OF PROCEEDINGS.

Resolved, That a correct copy of the proceedings of this Convention be prepared by the Secretary, E. O. Perrin, and certified to by the President of this Convention, for publication by the resident committee at Washington City.

A delegate from Massachusetts. I rise to make an amendment to the motion of adournment. It is, that when this Convention adjourns it shall adjourn with three cheers for the Constitution and the Union of our fathers, three cheers for the President of the United States, and three cheers for this Convention, that signalizes a permanent and enduring Union for all time. [Applause.]

THE PRESIDENT. Before putting that motion the Chair desires to announce that a note has been received from Hon. Mr. Dix, Major General, who presided in the preliminary proceedings of this Convention, which will be read. [Enthusiastic applause.] The Secretary then read the note, as follows:

NOTE FROM GENERAL DIX.

WIGWAM, *August* 15, 1866.

To Saml. J. Tilden, Esq., Chairman of the New York Delegation:

DEAR SIR: I am obliged to return to New York this afternoon on urgent business. The admirable spirit of harmony and conciliation which pervades the Convention renders my presence unnecessary, and leaves me no other regret than that of being unable to witness the close of the proceedings so auspiciously commenced and so full of promise for future good.

Very truly yours,

J. A. DIX.

[Loud cheering and applause.]

THANKS TO THE CONVENTION BY THE PRESIDENT.

THE PRESIDENT. Gentlemen of the Convention: For the kindness and courtesy with which you have sustained the Chair, and to which, by your resolution, you have been pleased to allude, I return you my sincere thanks. Before putting that motion, which shall terminate the proceeding of this Convention, I shall ask you once more to join with the Rev. Mr. Elliott in invoking the benedictions of Almighty God, by whose support we are sure of success, but without which we shall inevitably fail.

Rev. Mr. Elliott then advanced to the front of the stage and delivered the following prayer:

THE CLOSING PRAYER.

O Thou Great Ruler of the Universe and Author of all peace, and order, and harmony, and law in earth and Heaven, it is meet and right that we should bow our hearts before Thee on this deeply interesting occasion, and offer thanks to Thee, the Great Preserver of men and of nations, that we have been permitted to meet together after the confusion of years, under such favorable auspices, surrounded and protected by that Providence and by that disposition of order and law that is now about us. We recognize Thy gracious Providence, and offer thanks to Thee, the Author of all our mercies. We thank Thee that Thou hast put it into the hearts of these Thy servants to come together and to organize themselves into harmony from the various parts of this Union, and once more to take the friendly hand and pass the friendly greeting with each other in Thy presence, and to renew with hearty sincerity their friendships here on earth. O Lord God of our fathers, who planted us, who built us up, who made us great, and kept us united, and by whose gracious will and providence we are again one people, we offer thanks to Thee for the harmony of this body, for the union of hearts that has been manifested throughout this Convention; for that conciliation of spirit that has been seen in all its members and all its proceedings. We thank God for the blessings that now crown our nation, and especially for the President of the United States, who is so worthy of his situation and position. O Lord God Almighty, who raiseth and sustaineth those that are in authority, let Thy blessings come upon him, and sustain him in his difficult and arduous task, that he may carry out to complete success the plan by which we may become one united and great people now and perpetually. May the blessing of God rest upon all the committees and upon all the resolutions and addresses, and upon all the arrangements by which these Thy servants propose to carry out the principles of the Union. O Lord God, do Thou go with them to their several States and direct them in all their work. Be with us and remain with us through life, and when life is done, may we meet in that place above, where union is the law that pervades the society, and where, united, we shall reign immortal. These, with all other blessings, grant us, for the sake of Him that lived and died to save us, and to Father, Son, and Holy Ghost we will ascribe praise due now and forever. And may the blessings of Almighty God, Father, Son, and Holy Ghost, rest upon this Convention, upon this nation, upon its rulers, now and forever. Amen.

THE SECRETARY. I have to announce to the Convention that, as many of the names given to the various committees have not been distinctly heard, we will hold a session at room 44, at the Continental Hotel, for the purpose of obtaining all names corrected upon the proper committees before they receive the offical signature of the President of this Convention. We will be in session all the afternoon and to-night there.

THE FINAL ADJOURNMENT.

THE PRESIDENT. The motion is that this Convention do now adjourn without day. Those in favor of that motion say Aye—unanimous. Those opposed No—none. It is carried, and the Chair does now pronounce this Convention adjourned without day.

The wildest enthusiasm ensued, hearty and prolonged cheering being given for the Union, for President Johnson, and for the triumphant succes of the Convention.

A correct copy of abridged edition.

J. R. DOOLITTLE, *President.*

E. O. PERRIN, *Secretary.*

The Hon. REVERDY JOHNSON, Chairman of the Committee appointed to wait on the President of the United States to present him with an authentic copy of the Proceedings of the National Union Convention, made the following remarks previous to presenting the same:

SPEECH OF THE HON. REVERDY JOHNSON.

MR. PRESIDENT: We are before you as a Committee of the National Union Convention, which met in Philadelphia on Tuesday, the 14th instant, charged with the duty of presenting you with an authenticated copy of its proceedings.

Before placing it in your hands, will you permit us to congratulate you that, in the object for which the Convention was called, in the enthusiasm with which in every State and Territory, the call was responded to, in the unbroken harmony of its deliberations, in the unanimity with which the principles it has declared were adopted, and more especially in the patriotic and constitutional character of the principles themselves, we are confident that you and the country will find gratifying and cheering evidence that there exists among the people a public sentiment which renders an early and complete restoration of the Union, as established by the Constitution, certain and inevitable.

Party faction, seeking the continuance of its misrule, may momentarily delay it, but the principles of political liberty, for which our forefathers successfully contended, and to secure which they adopted the Constitution, are so glaringly inconsistent with the condition in which the country has been placed by such misrule, that it will not be permitted a much longer duration.

We wish, Mr. President, you could have personally witnessed the spirit of concord and brotherly affection which animated every member of the Convention. Great as your confidence ever has been in the intelligence and patriotism of your fellow-citizens, in their deep devotion to the Union, and in their present determination to reinstate and maintain it, that confidence would have become a positive conviction if you could have seen and heard all that was done and said upon the occasion. Every heart was evidently full of joy; every eye beamed with patriotic animation. Despondency gave place to assurance that our late dreadful civil strife, ended, the blissful reign of peace, under the protection, not of arms, but of the Constitution and Laws, would have sway, and be in every part of our land cheerfully acknowledged, and in perfect good faith obeyed, you would not have doubted that the recurrence of dangerous domestic insurrection in the future is not to be apprehended. If you could have seen, sir, the men of Massachusetts and South Carolina coming into the Convention on the first day of its meeting, hand in hand, amidst the rapturous applause of the whole body, awakened by heartfelt gratification at the event, filling the eyes of thousands with tears of joy, which they neither could nor desired to suppress, you would have felt as every person present felt, that the time had arrived when all sectional or other perilous dissension had ceased, and that nothing would be heard in the future but the voice of harmony, proclaiming devotion to a common country, pride in being bound together by a common Union, established and protected by forms of government proved by experience to be eminently fitting for the exigencies of either war or peace.

In the principles announced by the Convention, and in the feeling there manifested, we have every assurance that harmony throughout our entire land will soon prevail. We know that, as in former days, as was eloquently said by Webster, the nation's most gifted orator and statesman, Massachusetts and South Carolina went "shoulder to shoulder through the Revolution," and stood hand in hand "round the Administration of Washington, and felt his own great arm lean on them for support," so will they again, with like unanimity, devotion, and power, stand round your Administration, and cause you to feel that you may also lean on them for support. In the proceedings, Mr. President, which we are to place in your hands, you will find that the Convention performed the grateful duty imposed upon them by their knowledge of your "devotion to the Constitution, the laws, and interest of your country," as illustrated by your entire Presidential career, of declaring that in you they "recognize a Chief Magistrate worthy of the nation, and equal to the great crisis upon which your lot is cast." And in this declaration it gives us unmixed pleasure to add, we are confident that the Convention have but spoken the intelligent and patriotic opinion of the country. Ever inaccessible to the low influences which often control the mere partizan, governed alone by an honest opinion of Constitutional obligations and rights, and of the duty of looking solely to the true interest, safety, and honor of the nation, such a class is incapable of resorting to any stale bait for popularity at the expense of the public good.

In the measures which you have adopted for the restoration of the Union, the Convention saw only a continuance of the policy which, for the same purpose, was inaugurated by your immediate predecessor. In his re-election by the people, after that policy had been fully indicated and had been made one of the issues of the contest, those of his political friends who are now assailing you for strictly pursuing it are forgetful or regardless of the opinions which their support of his re-election necessarily involved. Being upon the same ticket with that much-lamented public servant, whose foul assassination touched the heart of the civilized world with grief and horror, you would have been false to obvious duty if you had not endeavored to carry out the same policy. And, judging now by the opposite one which Congress has pursued, its wisdom and patriotism are vindicated by the fact that that of Congress has but continued a broken Union by keeping ten of the States in which at one time the insurrection existed, as far as they could accomplish it, in the condition of subjugated provinces, denying to them the right to be represented whilst subjecting their people to every species of legislation, including taxation. That such a state of things is at war with the very genius of our Government, inconsistent with every idea of political freedom, and most perilous to the peace and safety of the country, no reflecting man can fail to believe. We hope, sir, that the proceedings of the Convention will cause you to adhere, if possible, with even greater firmness to the cause which you are pursuing by satisfying you that the people are with you, and that the wish which lies nearest to their heart is that a perfect restoration of our Union at the earliest moment be attained, and a conviction that that result can only be accomplished by the measures which you are pursuing; and, in the discharge of the duties which these impose upon you, we, as did every member of the Convention, again, for ourselves, individually tender you "our profound respect and assurance of our cordial and sincere support."

With a reunited Union, with no foot but that of a freeman treading, or permitted to tread our soil, with industry renewed, with a Nation's faith pledged forever to a strict observance of all its obligations, with kindness and fraternal love everywhere prevailing, the desolations of war will soon be removed, its sacrifices of life, sad as they have been, will, with a Christian resignation, be referred to a Providential purpose of fixing our beloved country on a firm and endurable basis, which will forever place our liberty and happiness beyond the reach of human peril.

Then, too, and forever will our Government challenge the admiration and receive the respect of the Nations of the World, and be in no danger of any effort to impair our rights, or to impeach our honor; and permit me, sir, in conclusion, to add that, great as is your solicitude for the restoration of our domestic peace, and engrossing as are your labors to that end, we rejoice to see that you keep also a watchful eye upon the rights of the Nation; and that, as far as depends upon you, any attempt by an assumed or actual foreign power to enforce an illegal blockade "against the Government or citizens of the United States" (to use your own mild but expressive words) "will be disallowed."

In this determination I am sure I speak but the voice of the Nation when I say that you will receive the unanimous approval of your fellow-citizens. Now, sir, as the Chairman of this Committee, and in behalf of the Convention, I have the honor to present you with an authenticated copy of its proceedings.

The PRESIDENT replied as follows:

REPLY O

Mr. Chairman and Gentlemen of the Co

Language is inadequate to express t

sion. Perhaps I could express more by permitting silence to speak and you to infer what I ought to say. I confess that, notwithstanding the experience I have had in public life, and the audiences I have addressed, this occasion and this assemblage are calculated to, and do, overwhelm me. As I have said, I have not language to convey adequately my present feelings and emotions.

In listening to the address which your eloquent and distinguished chairman has just delivered, the proceedings of the Convention, as they transpired, recurred to my mind. Seemingly, I partook of the inspiration that prevailed in the Convention when I received a despatch, sent by two of its distinguished members, conveying in terms the scene which has just been described, of South Carolina and Massachusetts, arm in arm, marching into that vast assemblage, and thus giving evidence that the two extremes had come together again, and that for the future they were united, as they had been in the past, for the preservation of the Union. When I was thus informed that in that vast body of men, distinguished for intellect and wisdom, every eye was suffused with tears on beholding the scene, I could not finish reading the despatch to ne associated with me in the office, for my own feelings overcame me. [Applause.] think we may justly conclude that we are acting under a proper inspiration, and hat we need not be mistaken that the finger of an overruling and unerring Providence in this great movement.

The nation is in peril. We have just passed through a mighty, a bloody, a momentus ordeal, and yet do not find ourselves free from the difficulties and dangers that at rst surrounded us. While our brave soldiers, both officers and men, [turning to General Grant, who stood on the right,] have by their heroism won laurels imperishable, there are still greater and more important duties to perform; and while we have had their coöperation in the field, now that they have returned to civil pursuits, we need their support in our efforts to restore the Government and perpetuate peace. [Applause.] So far as the Executive Department of the Government is concerned, the effort has been made to restore the Union, to heal the breach, to pour oil into the wounds which were consequent upon the struggle, and (to speak in common phrase) to prepare, as the learned and wise physician would a plaster, healing in character and coextensive with the wound. [Applause.] We thought, and we think, that we had partially succeeded; but as the work progresses, as reconciliation seemed to be taking place, and the country was becoming reunited, we found a disturbing and marring element opposing us. In alluding to that element, I shall go no further than your Convention and the distinguished gentleman who has delivered to me the report of its proceedings. I shall make no reference to it that I do not believe the time and the occasion justify.

We have witnessed in one department of the Government every endeavor to prevent the restoration of peace, harmony, and Union. We have seen hanging upon the verge of the Government, as it were, a body called, or which assumes to be, the Congress of the United States, while in fact it is a Congress of only a part of the States. We have seen this Congress pretend to be for the Union, when its every step and act tended to perpetuate disunion and make a disruption of the States inevitable. Instead of promoting reconciliation and harmony, its legislation has partaken of the character of penalties, retaliation, and revenge. This has been the course and policy of one portion of your Government.

The humble individual who is now addressing you stands the representative of another department of the Government. The manner in which he was called upon to occupy that position I shall not allude to on this occasion. Suffice it to say, that he is here under the Constitution of the country, and being here by virtue of its provisions, he takes his stand upon that charter of our liberties as the great rampart of civil and religious liberty. [Prolonged cheering.] Having been taught in my early life to hold it sacred, and having done so during my whole public career, I shall ever continue to reverence the Constitution of my fathers, and to make it my guide. [Hearty applause.]

I know it has been said (and I must be permitted to indulge in the remark) that the Executive Department of the Government has been despotic and tyrannical. Let me ask this audience of distinguished gentlemen to point to a vote I ever gave, to a speech I ever made, to a single act of my whole public life that has not been against tyranny and despotism. What position have I ever occupied—what ground have I ever assumed where it can be truthfully charged that I failed to advocate the amelioration and elevation of the great masses of my countrymen? [Cries of "Never," and great applause.]

So far as charges of this kind are concerned, they are simply intended to delude the public mind into the belief that it is not the designing men who make such accusations, but some one else in power who is usurping and trampling upon the rights and perverting the principles of the Constitution. It is done by them for the purpose of covering their own acts. ["That's so," and applause;] and I have felt it my duty, in vindication of principle, to call the attention of my countrymen to their proceedings. When we come to examine who has been playing the part of the tyrant, by whom do we find despotism exercised? As to myself, the elements of my nature, the pursuits of my life, have not made me either in my feelings or in my practice aggressive. My nature, on the contrary, is rather defensive in its character; but having taken my stand upon the broad principles of liberty and the Constitution, there is not power enough on earth to drive me from it. [Loud and prolonged applause.] Having placed myself upon that broad platform, I have not been awed or dismayed or intimidated by either threats or encroachments, but have stood there in conjunction with patriotic spirits, sounding the tocsin of alarm when I deemed the citadel of liberty in danger. [Great applause.]

I said on a previous occasion, and repeat now, that all that was necessary in this great contest against tyranny and despotism was that the struggle should be sufficiently audible for the American people to hear and properly understand the issues it involved. They did hear, and looking on and seeing who the contestants were, and what the struggle was about, determined that they would settle this question on the side of the Constitution and of principle. [Cries of "That's so," and applause.] I proclaim here to-day, as I have on previous occasions, that my faith is in the great mass of the people. In the darkest moment of this struggle, when the clouds seemed to be most lowering, my faith, instead of giving way, loomed up through their gloom; for, beyond, I saw that all would be well in the end. My countrymen, we all know that, in the language of Thomas Jefferson, tyranny and despotism can be exercised and exerted more effectually by the many than the one. We have seen Congress gradually encroach step by step upon constitutional rights, and violate, day after day and month after month, fundamental principles of the Government. [Cries of "That's so," and applause.] We have seen a Congress that seemed to forget that there was a limit to the sphere and scope of legislation. We have seen a Congress in a minority assume to exercise power which, if allowed to be consummated, would result in despotism or monarchy itself. [Enthusiastic applause.] This is truth, and because others, as well as myself, have seen proper to appeal to the patriotism and republican feeling of the country, we have been denounced in the severest terms. Slander upon slander, vituperation upon vituperation of the most virulent character, has made its way through the press. What, gentlemen, has been your and my sin? What has been the cause of our offending? I will tell you: Daring to stand by the Constitution of our fathers.

Mr. Chairman, I consider the proceedings of this Convention equal to, if not more important than those of any convention that ever assembled in the United States. [Great applause.] When I look upon that collection of citizens coming together voluntarily, and sitting in council with ideas, with principles and views commensurate with all the States, and co-extensive with the whole people, and contrast it with a Congress whose policy, if persisted in, will destroy the country, I regard it as more important than any Convention that has sat—at least since 1787. [Renewed applause.] I think I may also say that the declarations that were there made are equal to those contained in the Declaration of Independence itself, and I here to-day pronounce them a second Declaration of Independence. [Cries of "Glorious," and most enthusiastic and prolonged applause.] Your address and declarations are nothing more nor less than a reaffirmation of the Constitution of the United States. [Cries of "Good," and applause.]

Yes, I will go farther, and say that the declarations you have made, that the principles you have enunciated in your address, are a second proclamation of emancipation to the people of the United States. [Renewed applause.] For, in proclaiming and reproclaiming these great truths, you have laid down a constitutional platform on which all, without reference to party, can make common cause, engage in a common effort to break the tyranny which the dominant party in Congress has so relentingly exercised, and stand united together for the restoration of the States and the preservation of the Government. The question only is the salvation of the country; for our country rises above all party consideration or influences. [Cries of "Good," and applause.] How many are there in the United States that now require to be free? They have the shackles upon their limbs and are bound as rigidly by the behests of party leaders in the National Congress as though they were in fact in slavery. I repeat, then, that your declaration is the second proclamation of emancipation to the people of the United States, and offers a common ground upon which all patriots can stand. [Applause.]

In this connexion, Mr. Chairman and gentlemen, let me ask what have I to gain more than the advancement of the public welfare? I am as much opposed to the indulgence of egotism as any one; but here, in a conversational manner, while formally receiving the proceedings of this Convention, I may be permitted again to inquire what I have gained, except one thing—the consummation of the great work of restoration? My race is nearly run. I have been placed in the high office which I occupy by the Constitution of the country, and I may say that I have held, from lowest to highest, almost every station to which a man may attain in our Government. I have passed through every position, from Alderman of a village to the Presidency of the United States. And surely, gentlemen, this should be enough to gratify a reasonable ambition.

If I had wanted authority, or if I had wished to perpetuate my own power, how easily could I have held and wielded that which was placed in my hands by the measure called the Freedmen's Bureau Bill! [Laughter and applause.] With an army which it placed at my discretion I could have remained at the Capital of the Nation, and with fifty or sixty millions of appropriations at my disposal, with the machinery to be unlocked by my own hands, with my satraps and dependents in every town and village, with the Civil Rights Bill following as an auxiliary, [laughter,] and with the patronage and other appliances of the Government, I could have proclaimed myself Dictator. ["That's true!" and applause.]

But, gentlemen, my pride and my ambition have been to occupy that position which retains all power in the hands of the people. [Great cheering.] It is upon them I have always relied: it is upon them I rely now. [A voice: "And the people will not disappoint you."] And I repeat, that neither the taunts nor jeers of Congress, nor of a subsidized, calumniating press, can drive me from [illegible]pose. [Great applause.] I acknowledge no superior except my God, the author [illegible]y existence, and the people of the United States. [Prolonged an[illegible]ic chee[illegible]ing.] The commands of th[illegible] one I try to obey as best I can, com[illegible]oor humanity. As to the other, in a political and representative sense, the high behests of the people have always been, and ever will be, respected and obeyed by me. [Applause.]

Mr. Chairman, I have said more than I intended to say. For the kind allusion to myself, contained in your address, I thank you. In this crisis, and at the present period of my public life, I hold above all price, and shall ever recur with feelings of profound gratification, to the resolution containing the endorsement of a convention emanating spontaneously from the great mass of the people. With conscientious conviction as my courage, the Constitution as my guide, and my faith in the people, I trust and hope that my future action may be such that you and the Convention you represent may not regret the assurance of confidence you have so generously expressed. ["We are sure of it."]

Before separating, my friends, one and all, please accept my heartfelt thanks for the kind manifestations of regard and respect you have exhibited on this occasion.

NATIONAL UNION EXECUTIVE COMMITTEE, *August* 22, 1866.

The Chairmain of the National Union Executive Committee, in conformity with a resolution adopted at a meeting of the Committee, held at Philadelphia, August 16, 1866, appoints the following members of the Committee to constitute a Sub-Committee, with power to act in matters relating to the pending campaign:

COL. JAMES P. BABCOCK, New Haven, Conn.
HON. ROBERT H. PRUYN, Albany, N. Y.
GEN. SAMUEL M. ZULICK, Philadelphia, Pa.
HON. THOS. G. PRATT, Baltimore, Md.
HON. JESSE O. NORTON, Chicago, Ill.
BARTON ABLE, Esq., St. Louis, Mo.
HON. WM. L. SHARKEY, Jackson, Miss.

JOSEPH T. CROWELL,
Chairman National Union Executive Committee,
RAHWAY, N. J.

NOTE.—On account of the urgent demand for the Proceedings of the Convention, an abridged edition can only be published at this time.

The full Proceedings, containing a list of Delegates, with letters of Hon. Robert C. Winthrop, Thomas Ewing, William C. Rives, and others, will be issued in pamphlet form at as early a date as practicable.

E. O. PERRIN,
Secretary National Union Convention.

www.ingramcontent.com/pod-product-compliance
Lightning Source LLC
LaVergne TN
LVHW011128110826
845150LV00008B/2274

* 9 7 8 1 4 1 8 1 9 5 3 3 5 *